LIBIDINES
EXONIENSES

OR

The Lusts and Desires of
THE
MEN of EXETER

herein set fforth in divers Questions
& **LETTERS**

WISE, WITTY, PLAINTIVE, PITHY, SAD,
SVPERCILIOVS, QVEER, QVERVLOVS,
MERRY, MOVRNFVL, LAMENTABLE,
LEWD, &c, &c

wherein is displaid all that is wrong
with this Colledge and its several
INHABITANTS;

with ANSWERS thereto by the
BVRRASAHIB KVMAR GVRAM
an Hindoo;

"Ask and it shall be given unto
you."

AO: DOII:
MCMLV

ye fforth quad

ye Bursar

Chaps

Perversion

Religion

Lights

ye art ffund

Sex

Wogs

Musick

Darts

ye scholars Table

1

Acknowledgements

A special thanks to Professor Marilyn Butler for suggesting the idea for this book, and John Speirs and John Leighfield for editing the publication.

Additional thanks to (alphabetically) Alan Bennett, John Boulter, Frances Cairncross, Will Canestaro, Richard Chapman, Judith Curthoys, Sam Eadie, David Garrood, Martin Grosvenor, Katrina Hancock, Jessica Houlgrave, Tim Padfield, Ari Romney, John Roper, John Saunders, Memo Spathis, Andrew Speirs, Susan Speirs, Elizabeth Spicer, Peter Thomas, David Vaisey, and Laurelle Vingoe.

Table of Contents

Foreword by the Rector

The JCR Suggestion Book was, in the golden years of the late 1950s, a work of both literary genius and scurrilous schoolboy humour. The impetus to publish it came from my predecessor, Professor Marilyn Butler, who enthusiastically promoted the idea. Without her, it would never have happened. Two Old Members, John Speirs and John Leighfield, have generously done much to prepare it.

Alan Bennett, who wrote many of the funniest entries, has kindly contributed a foreword - on the clear understanding that it should not be reprinted elsewhere. So, in acquiring a copy of this little book, you have a rare treat - a genuine limited edition. You also have some passages that are not for those with delicate susceptibilities. If you are easily shocked, avoid the penultimate chapter, which we have included because - well, that's what Exeter students were like in the 1950s. If you were one of them, you will understand.

Frances Cairncross

Foreword

This is none of my doing. I never thought as I lazed in an armchair in Exeter JCR [Junior Common Room] in 1958 that my idle doodlings would return half a century later to remind me of my younger self.

It's a self I was never entirely happy with at the time and find embarrassing in recollection, and indeed I once imagined a plot in which a series of seemingly random and unconnected murders turned out to be all of persons who had known the murderer in his youth. It came from the heart; to be confronted on the brink of old age with one's youthful self is no treat.

However. To look through this book is also to be reminded of how gifted some of my contemporaries were. Brian Brindley's Gothick confections are splendid creations and done at a time when this style of illustration and architecture was not highly thought of and so, besides being funny, was also pioneering. John Morley's too are remarkable, though he lacks Brindley's exuberant fantasy. Both, though, spent immense care on their contributions, deep in concentration in a corner of the JCR with the Suggestions Book on their knees. As always, their drawings were done *in situ*. I don't think the Book ever left the Common Room and maybe wasn't supposed to.

Great diligence went into their productions and, except where law was concerned, Brindley was conscientious to an extraordinary degree. There is some evidence in the book of his infatuation with Ogilvy, a blond rugger-playing hearty which, for the purposes of the Suggestions Book at least, Brindley inflated into a *grande passion*. On one occasion in the middle of the night armed with his John Bull printing outfit Brindley stole down to the Back Quad where the bogs were situated. There were some twenty or so lavatories, each loo furnished with boxes of interleaved Izal lavatory paper, a hundred or so sheets to a box. Brindley painstakingly disassembled each box, stamped "Oggers is Lovely" on every sheet, before putting the boxes together again. If genius is an infinite capacity for taking pains, this was it.

Also remarkable in a different way are the cartoons of Derek Whitelock. I'd known Whitelock during National Service when we'd been together on the Joint Service Russian Course. I had been in the same bedroom and barrack room with him for nearly two years. We were very different in temperament so we were both appalled when we arrived at Exeter in 1954 to find that with the best of intentions Rector Barber [Eric Arthur Barber, Rector, 1943-1956] had arranged that we should yet again share rooms. Fifty years later I can still remember my dismay.

It's not surprising therefore that at the time I seldom found Whitelock's contributions funny but I'm happy at this late date to make amends. His cartoons are done in a style that anticipates Nicholas Garland's *Private Eye* comic strip on Barry Mackenzie. They're full of private jokes (as indeed many of the letters are) and this blunts their impact, but they're so individual and lively one feels that when he went to Australia he may have missed his way.

The Common Room in which these contributions were written or drawn merits a mention as, like many Oxford Junior Common Rooms in the fifties, it boasted some excellent pictures, bought yearly out of the JCR Art Fund. So there were paintings by John Minton, Michael Ayrton, David Jones and Augustus John, some of them superb. There was no thought then that these were potentially of great value and we just took them for granted... as indeed we did the engraved seventeenth-century silver tankards in which beer was served in Hall.

That relaxed and unregulated atmosphere ended in the late sixties when many of the paintings were casualties of the student unrest of those years (and some of the tankards too). For that and other reasons I am thankful to have been an undergraduate in a more trusting and carefree age of which this book is a funny and also a melancholy reminder.

Alan Bennett (1954, Modern History)

Sir,

Mr. Bonnett appears to be adopting a singularly mournful costume nowadays.

Why?

Yours etc J.H Morley.

(Michaelmas '57)

Note by the Editors

In 1993 Dr Marilyn Butler was elected Rector of Exeter College, Oxford and thus became the first female Head of a former all-male Oxford College. In July 1994 she presided at a Gaudy (an Oxford reunion) for former undergraduates who had commenced their career at Exeter in the years 1956-1959 (when she herself had been an undergraduate at St Hilda's College, Oxford). In preparing for her speech at dinner she took the advice of a colleague, who suggested that she would learn something about those attending the dinner from the Junior Common Room Suggestion Books (JCR Books) for the years 1956-59, which had gained a reputation as the golden age.

The JCR Books had for many years been used to bring suggestions and complaints to the attention of the annual Presidents of the JCR. Normally it would take a year at a minimum for a book to be filled. However, in the early '50s two major changes occurred: undergraduates started writing to the President on any subject which took their fancy, and a few of them started adding drawings to their letters. Zander Wedderburn's period as President in 1957-58 was the peak year, when five books were filled, including 148 drawings. By the time Roger Thorn became President in 1960, output was one and a half books and no drawings. After 6 years the golden age of the JCR Books was at an end.

In the late '90s we had cause to meet the Rector again in Oxford, when she raised the idea of publishing a short book with gems from the golden age of the JCR Books. Although Exeter is the fourth oldest college in Oxford, having been founded in 1314, it has never been as well known as the larger and wealthier colleges. The new Rector was keen to raise Exeter's profile and enhance its reputation as one of the most attractive of the middle-sized colleges for new undergraduates. An Oxford guide, shepherding visitors round Oxford, had been overheard explaining to his group outside the Exeter JCR that this was where Alan Bennett had studied and contributed to its golden age. It was this bit of information which suggested that there might be a readership beyond the graduates of the College itself, let alone the declining number of original contributors. Discussions with other Oxford (and Cambridge) graduates suggested that Exeter's JCR Books in the 1950s were indeed unusual if not unique. At any rate the outcome was that we agreed at another Gaudy in 2001 to take the lead with some colleagues in putting together a book reflecting Exeter College in the period 1952-1960.

Marilyn Butler retired in 2004 and was succeeded as Rector by Frances Cairncross. The original goal to provide an unusual and entertaining insight into aspects of life in an Oxford college and thus raise Exeter's profile and enhance its reputation has remained. Of course there have been radical changes since the 1950s, in particular the change from an all-male to a mixed college.

Some readers may therefore find this book of interest for historical reasons. The original expectation was that the letters would provide a fairly broad picture of life at Exeter in the 50s, requiring only a small amount of editorial explanation. This expectation has proved to be unrealistic, except perhaps for contemporary undergraduates who have retained their memory. The picture that is reflected in this book is not complete, because it only reflects what the undergraduates chose to write about. Their letters were ephemeral and not written with an eye to posterity. Indeed there was no requirement for completed JCR books to be retained.

However all but one seem to have survived.

It was also hoped that the letters could be reproduced as they are in the JCR Books. This too was quickly seen to be unrealistic. The letters were hand-written, and there was no attempt to ensure that they could be read easily, or even at all. Letters in the latter category tended to be written late in the evening after returning from a pub. The drawings are another matter. In many cases the accompanying text or letter can be shown as it was written.

The letters and drawings have been chosen from the relevant 20 JCR Books between 1952 & 1960. Seven of the chapters in the book are devoted to particular themes and allied sub-themes. Chapter 1 is about the JCR itself, Chapter 2 about the JCR Books, Chapter 4 about College Life, Chapter 7 about College Amenities, Chapter 9 about Extra-curricular Activities, Chapter 10 about what might now be considered Politically Incorrect subjects, and Chapter 11 about College Animals. The other four chapters are devoted to the three main contributors of drawings - Brian Brindley, Derek Whitelock and John Morley, plus Alan Bennett who drew himself from time to time and was regularly drawn by John Morley. However, drawings are scattered throughout all the chapters. For example there are six by John Morley in Chapter 1, since they fit the theme of the JCR. Some of the material in this book, especially in Chapter 10, is undoubtedly offensive. We have included it partly to give the true flavour of the Suggestion Book, and also because, among the crudeness, there are genuine pearls. Those of a delicate disposition should skip the penultimate chapter.

The 20 JCR Books are made up of 3,400 pages, of which the half on the right-hand side were for undergraduates' comments and the half on the left-hand side were for the Presidents of the JCR to respond. This book has just over 150 pages, made up of letters and drawings by the undergraduates, occasional responses by Presidents, and a short explanatory introduction to each chapter by the editors. All of the contributors, as well as those merely mentioned in passing, are indexed at the end of the book. The confusion in the Archive numbers reflects the lack of dates in the JCR Books, and their haphazard return to the Librarian by some of the Presidents. However it has been possible to allocate each letter and drawing or group of letters to the appropriate university term: Michaelmas (autumn), Hilary (spring) and Trinity (summer). Within each chapter and its sub-themes, where relevant, the letters and drawings have generally been included in chronological order. An exception would be where it makes sense to have two drawings facing each other.

J.G. Speirs (1956, Literae Humaniores)
J.P. Leighfield (1958, Literae Humaniores)

Chapter 1
The Junior Common Room (JCR)

For many undergraduates the JCR is the focal point of College life – not only for those living in college but also as a haven for those living out in rented accommodation. At Exeter, undergraduates visited the large room in order to talk, to argue, to play darts, to play shove-halfpenny (shovers), to read the newspapers and magazines, to read or write a letter in the JCR Book, and generally to pass the time, including sleeping. Friday and Saturday evenings, after 10pm, were often the noisiest periods, when members returned in various stages of inebriation and thus ready to engage in general mayhem. Simon Clements' drawing presents the final stage of exhaustion. All undergraduates were members of the Stapeldon Society (named after the College's founder), which met in the JCR every second Sunday evening during term-time. Each year the members elected a President, Secretary and Treasurer, plus a number of others to key posts. Some examples were: the Millerian Professor (named after Max Miller of Music Hall fame) whose job was to pass on gossip and tell dirty jokes and amusing stories at the fortnightly meetings; the LHCPE (Lord High Commissioner for Public Easement) whose job was to deal with complaints about the state of the baths and lavatories; the Captain of Punts; the three members of the Kitchen Committee, who discussed the quality of the meals with the Bursar and Chef once a fortnight; and the three members of the Art Committee.

All undergraduates contributed financially to the Society, and much of the money was distributed to many other College societies and clubs (vide Chapter 9). The provision of money to the Art Committee each year to buy paintings for the JCR regularly led to dissension. The members of the Stapeldon Society were usually sensible enough to elect to the Committee someone who was knowledgeable about art, someone else who was likely to support him, and a third person who spoke for the common man, i.e. the sporting and drinking fraternity. As the following letters show, the paintings of "The Passing of Venus" by Burne-Jones (who was at Exeter with William Morris) and "The Orange Girl" were not received well – although in the former case the "common man" supported the purchase, drawing the Society's attention to the painting's many wonderful points, starting with Venus's breasts. This painting was sold many years later at a huge profit, which provided large funds for the Boat Club and other College societies (but not to buy other paintings).

The other letters and the drawings are self-explanatory, except those about Big Business. This was a large metal sculpture, which normally resided behind a sofa in the JCR. The members of the Adelphi Society (a privately elected dining club, which tended to reflect private rather than state education) were inclined to end their annual festivities in college by threatening or occasionally endeavouring unsuccessfully to throw Big Business from the top of the College Tower. Its current location is unknown.

The chapter finishes with a short poem by John Moat. As he became President of the JCR shortly afterwards, it shows that raising the cultural tone was appreciated.

Your presence was undoubtedly missed this night.
What action do you propose to take to suppress
debauchery, rancid and rampant, or would Exeter
not be the same without it?

Yrs, etc. Simon Clements

(Michaelmas '55)

Sir,

The shovers board should be as sacrosanct as the wicket at Lord's or the Centre Court at Wimbledon. Have younger men no respect for the arena which was the scene of many a triumph for Mr. De Salis – incomparably the finest player yet produced by Stapeldon's foundation?

Yours etc,
John Party
(Michaelmas '52)

⟨ ⟩

Sir,

Mr. Wells-Furby declares that the J.C.R. carpet is as sandy

as Blackpool beach.

Should he not take advantage of the fine weather we are enjoying? I am sure that the President would not object to the improvisation of a temporary swimming-pool in the fireplace

Yours sincerely,
J. H. Morley.

(Trinity '57)

⟨ ⟩

Sir,

Mr. Bennett says we ought to have a stove in the J.C.R. so that we can cook things.

Yours etc JHMorley.

(Hilary '58)

[R. Ben Jones was the Amelia Jackson Senior Scholar, a coveted scholarship, and was therefore a target for 'roasting'.]

Sir,

It is not often that I really object to a picture, but this latest manifestation of Mr. Morley's twisted sense of humour ('Venus's Passage?') is really the end. If it wasn't so large and garish I wouldn't mind, but the thing can be seen and distinctly – from nearly every part of the JCR. Could it, please, be relegated to the Morris Room? If we have to have such obscene nonsense in the college please let's keep it together and stop the JCR being ruined.

Yours,
JM Ashworth

P.S. While we're on it, what about the spring clean in the Morris Room.

Sir,

The Burne Jones is a very heavy picture. The carpenter had to hang it in the JCR: the plaster of the Morris Room wall would not take the weight without some considerable hacking about of the famous (sic) wallpaper.

The Morris Room is too dark for the picture to be seen. This is NOT, despite dissentients, an advantage. The temperature of the Morris room varies considerably during the winter, which would not be good for a panel.

Also, there is no earthly reason why a picture that was bought specifically for the JCR should be taken out of it in order to put it in an allegedly suitable setting. None of the pictures in the JCR are contemporary with the room.

Yours etc.,
JH Morley

Sir,

No pre-Raphaelite-ite worthy of his salt could do anything less or more than disagree with Mr.(sic) Morley. (I presume, though he has been ungracious enough to write anonymously, and not only that, to leave his letter unsigned). There is in fact (sic) every reason why the picture Venus Passing should be hung in the Morris Room. Morley, with his essentially superficial appreciation of the nature of pre-Raphaelite art, has not realised that its central idea is one of wholeness. The memory of Morris, Burne-Jones, Madox Ford, Rossetti, the lot, is not served by scattering their works abroad – some in here, some in the Morris Room, some in the chapel, some in the Forth. No. We would do better to put them all together – pictures, tapestries, aspidistras, curtains, nudes, Flora, Pomona, all of them in the Morris Room. That way we could appreciate the essential oneness (most of the pre-Raphaelites were, you know) of their art.

Suggest as a possible site for Venus Passing where the blackboard is now – then you could drill a tremendous screw into the door and fit it on there. All very appropriate. Mind you, it would have to be hung sideways but would be none the worse for that. Venus (passing) might take on new delights, newer from this new position.

The Old Merchant Taylor Haberdasher Askeians who are having their annual beano in the Morris Room this very moment (the sound of hearty Haberdasheraskeian merriment comes faintly through the wall as I write this) would, I think, be hardly displeased were we to add Venus Passing to the lascivious titbits (sic) which we all associate with Old Boys' Dinners.

Think how the Old Beak's (headmaster 1908-1948) eyes would twinkle. How many more old boys' beanos there would be. Let Venus pass into the Morris Room. She can do nothing but good there.

Yrs, etc,
Alan Bennett

Sir,

  I suggest some new pictures:
> "Monarch of the Glen"
> "The British Lion"
> "H.M. The Queen"

Yours,
K Rose

Sir,

  I don't know much about art (to coin a phrase) but the new pictures in the JCR call for a few comments. We should all feel free to do this because as was said a couple of pages back – we paid for 'em.

1. Black and white type at this end (near the Culver Memorial Painting). It is undoubtedly phallic, perhaps derivative in a bad sense of neo-phallicism.
2. The multicoloured one in the middle. Is this the latest in action painting? So far there have been paints thrown, trodden, trowelled, and ridden over – this I feel is more expressive though, as it seems to be a random cat-heave design. Ultra-modern, and possibly recording the artist's own criticism and feelings before he painted it.
3. The one by the dart board – which is pleasing in its simplicity, and relaxing in that it does not seem to 'say' anything – good or bad, clean or sordid – and thus must stand as a neutral work of art, expressive of the empty mind, and unencumbered by the entrammelled mind of genius, or angry-young-artist.

MJ Moffatt

President's reply,

  Mr Moffatt, please, a man who can employ words with such easeful mastery, elusive melancholy, should keep himself from commenting on other's creations.

AAI Wedderburn
(Trinity '58)

❧

Sir,

  The orange girl, or whatever it is, gets a bad press. Whenever the new paintings have been criticised over the last 2 years one is always told that the Captain of Arts knows his business and that these paintings are worth every penny and will accumulate in value, etc. etc. I don't dispute this. But capital accumulation is not the function of the Art Fund. We ought I think to buy pictures we shall enjoy, encouraging young artists etc etc. at the same time. (There must be some struggling artists who paint stuff that is enjoyable for the majority of people here?) Patently most people here don't like the orange splodge, and, for them, it has no aesthetic merit, however valuable or profound. Do you think, just occasionally, we can try new pictures that will give enjoyment to the JCR itself.

Phillip Whitehead

Dear Sir,

I agree with Mr. Whitehead. Let's have lots and lots of lovely mediocre paintings. Pictures that chaps can tell just what it is at a glance --. None of these things that look like a child's impression of something. This should turn out a lot cheaper too. The Art committee need not go on expeditions to London. They can just have a walk round to Boots and buy a few pictures that everyone but everyone will like. I might suggest:
(i) ducks flying over marshes
(ii) Spanish dancers in red frocks
(iii) The odd ballet dancer
(iv) A negress of greenish hue
And if the chaps glands stir a bit
(v) a proper nude showing all details in photographic exactness (untouched)
Then we'll have something of real value. "A thing of beauty is a joy forever".

John Meakin
(Michaelmas '60)

Sir,

I have now seen 'Playboy' for the first time in the JCR. In view of the fact that some lecherous s*d always removes the centre pages before the chaps get a chance, I suggest that the present policy of displaying the said pages on the JCR board for the gratification and titillation of all is very good news, and that the said policy is continued in perpetuum. By the way, Nigel Tub*s says the tot at present on view is deformed. Poor Mr. Tub*s. What do you think, Sir?

Yrs,
MA Spence

President's reply,

Bill Stone has been told to take out the centre pages in future and have them posted in the bar. I think one should realize that a woman's body is slightly different from the one we have been used to in the all-male world, which the British educational system imposes upon us. I'm told the German male does not regard the German female as being deformed. We might take a leaf out of their book.

Roger Thorn
(Michaelmas '60)

Sir,

It is said that, due to the unexpected disintegration of a trilobite, room has been found in the University Museum for past

Presidents of the J.C.R. It is said that you will have to desert yet another eager landlady.

Yrs etc JHMorley.

President's reply,
    Unlike Mr Bennett, I enjoy your drawings.

NR Graves
(Trinity '57)

Sir,

There is an indescribably anxious expression on Grave's face. He is biting his nails, picking his nose. He is flushed; his legs are twitching uncontrollably. Clouds of steam are issuing from his nostrils. At times a low, bitter laugh forces its way from between his lips. He says he is making a pig ~~about~~ of himself, & in reply to a question declares that he has read about the Schoolmaster. He is now passionately intertwining his fingers. He is picking his nose again. A question is again asked, & he says he has by no means finished. I, however, must finish this letter, for he has just handed me that intensely human document, that great social synopsis, the News of the World.

Yours &c JHMorley.

(Hilary '58)

Sir,

      Mr. Richard Johnson has been speaking to Mr. Alan Bennett, at the latter's earnest solicitation, of the last days in the Old Home, whereupon Messrs. Graves and Stambach showed all the signs of acute discomfort.

Yrs etc,
JH Morley

Sir,

      Nonsense. The above was caused by Mr. Coulson and others pissing on the fire.

Yrs etc,
AJ Bedson
(Hilary '58)

Sir,

Life is too easy these days. Students should live in garrets (no comments Staircase 8), smoke 'Gauloises' and die at an early age of cirrhosis and/or consumption. For preference they should eat only long cylindrical pieces of bread and foul cheese; and rather than take a 'Vac' job – horrible thought – sell their mistress to the D*ns. The NUS, sir, is the only link we have with our colourful, romantic past. Only the NUS officials can lead the corporate, duffle-coated student body against the last barriers of the 'Establishment', 'Subtopia', "Non-Union u –ism' 'Floods in the Fforth' and the other plagues of intellectual life. Of course the college should devote one third pence per head of the money given to the Government by the taxpayers who have given it to us to give to the NUS.

Vive la difference,
JM Ashworth

Sir,

May I support Peter Lewis's request that we join NUS? It is ten times cheaper if we join collectively, and by a strange co-incidence, ten times more expensive if you join individually. And they lay on several useful facilities, particularly for student travel but also in Grants battles, Vac jobs and Careers information. The idea used to be thrown out because NUS was connected with IUS which became Communist front, but now there is a separate non-Communist international co-ordinating body, and NUS is almost violently anti-Communist.

Yours etc,
AAI Wedderburn

Please Sir,
Who is NUS?
Yrs,
G Halliday

President's reply,

An organisation which provides/does not provide valuable/useless facilities for a moderate/exorbitant subscription and which for numerous good/bad reasons, we should/should not join.

NR Graves

Sir,

….I might add that most of the other colleges of the University are affiliated. When this argument was used by a pro-NUS orator in University College, he vehemently declared: "We should join, because Balliol is a member, Magdalen is a member, Lady Margaret Hall is a member, Jesus is a member…." But was interrupted by a languid American, who drawled: "Waal, if Jesus is a member, I guess I'll join too."
So should we.

Yours altruistically (I've paid my 15 shillings)
Sam Eadie
(Trinity '57)

Sir,

What is going on, please? The picture (by Romney) of the Hon: Dom: Dom: Parker (Earl of Macclesfield) that ought to hang on the screen in Hall, has vanished. Credible rumour informs me that it has been taken to the SCR for keeps. Is it reasonable that almost the only beautiful thing in an uninteresting and impoverished college should be immured where no-one but dons can ever see it. If this be true, which perhaps you might be able to find out, I am sure sufficiently high feelings might be aroused in the JCR to justify a suggestion that it should be put back where we can enjoy it. There is no call for them to be selfish – the noble earl was never a fellow, even if he did use the SCR. This is an outrage.

Yrs,

BDFT Brindley

President's reply,

It is true that the Hon: Dom: Dom: Parker is at present gracing the S.C.R. I began raising a fuss but soon found I hadn't a leg to stand on. When the gentleman in question – then Viscount Parker – graduated, he presented the picture to the Rector personally. It was loaned by a succeeding Rector to the Hall so that the undergraduates might view it for a time. However, this was only done on a temporary basis and now that the S.C.R. with the Rector's support has reasons for removing it from the Hall, it is perfectly justified in doing so.

E.R. Larsen
(Michaelmas '53)

Sir,

For the man about town **Ballerina**

FULLY FASHIONED **NYLON STOCKINGS**

FJ Roper
(Michaelmas '55)

Sir,

Why is the flag, presumably flying for Empire Day, at half-mast. Is this because we have left only half an Empire?

Really though, of all the outmoded reasons to fly a flag in 1955 Empire Day is about the worst! Anyway, why is Empire Day on May 24? It ought to be on April-Bloody-Fools Day.

Yours,
Robert Cook

Sir,

If only Mr Cook's intelligence – for which we all have the greatest respect – were equalled by his grasp of symbolism, he would see that there can be nothing more appropriate than the flying of the college flag at half-mast – a sign of penitence – on Empire Day. Still, sir, there are some of us who would be naked savages wandering around in the wilds of Lancashire were it not for the Roman Empire.

Yours sincerely,
JF Edge
(Trinity '55)

Sir,

The time has surely come when we should cease to be an exponent of Beaverbrook Imperialism. I am referring to the flying of the college flag, admittedly at not quite full mast, to celebrate Empire Day. The concept of Empire is nowadays a sentimental illusion that should be morally nauseating, not only to socialists. A protest should be registered with the flag-flying authorities.

Yrs etc,
Stephen Hatch

President's reply,

The college looks rather fine with the flag flying. I wish there were a few more days in the year when we could fly it.

NR Graves

Sir,

It is rather a good idea to give the college flag an airing now and then; I have not seen it before, and it looks rather fine fluttering above the Tower. Empire Day is as good an occasion as any to display it, too. I had not realized that half the country was 'morally nauseated' with the idea of Empire which I suppose shows how I have been misled by Beaverbrook Imperialism. Don't you feel proud, Sir, that Exeter, by flying its own flag, is flying 'the ultimate symbol of final and absolute disintegration of the Empire'? A staggering thought, isn't it? But let's go further next time, and fly the Hammer and Sickle.

Yours,
JG Speirs
(Trinity '57)

Dear Sir,

I have just been to a party (guess whose!). Like all parties, it looked like this. But it was very nice – really, I mean it. I saw you there, Sir – with a lady's (sic) shoe. I also saw John Moat, throwing a lady with great velocity over his shoulder. I also saw things that I would never repeat, Sir, even to you.

Yours etc,
John Morley

President's reply

Billy Smart Set. But nice little nooks. I only took one shoe. And the over-the-shoulder girl wasn't wearing any anyway.

I bet you repeat those naughty things at the next party.

AAI Wedderburn
(Michaelmas '57)

Sir,

On retiring last night I found my bed already occupied by 'Business'.

To those who tried to bring us together I publicly express my gratitude. I may say also that 'Business' has nothing on a brass monkey.

Yrs etc,

A Bennett

P.S. I take it also that this incident indicates that Business is regarded, by some members of the JCR at any rate, as a male animal.

(Hilary '56)

"I know not, Oh I know not, what joys await us there,
The pastures of the blessed are decked beyond compare."

Yours etc.

T Price Zimmerman

Sir,

I really do think that 'Big Business' should be brought out from behind the curtain in the Morris Room behind which it is lurking and placed in its wonted habit in the J.C.R. For, Sir, I think that 'Big Business' is a singularly appropriate symbol for this J.C.R. As you doubtless recall from your reading of the British novel of the century, Stella Gibbons' Cold Comfort Farm (this argument is 100% British made Sir), 'Big Business' is a bull, and a bull, Sir, is the perfect embodiment of the Exeter Junior Common Room. Not, sir, because of the product he so copiously exudes, oh no, sir, oh no! But rather, sir, for his incomparable <u>sexual prowess</u>. For it is a well-known fact, sir, that the Exeter Bulls are wont to romp the pastures of St. Hughs' and Lady Margaret Hall, and that due to their inordinate fondness for flowers (veritable Ferdinands they are, sir) many a once fair rose garden in St. Hilda's and Somerville now lieth desolate. So desolate, in fact, from the ruthless plucking of its blooms, that when Father Time cometh for the harvest, he shall find nought to reap but stalks and thorns. And this, sir, is the reason why the J.C.R. is so dull and empty a'nights, causing Mr. Coulson to lament the happier times.

Yours etc,

T Price Zimmerman

(Hilary '57)

Sir,

I've at last found out about Big Business. The whole truth has come to light! He's not just a pretty face you know, he's a politician! While browsing through the Labour party Handbook for 1951 I came across the following;

"Big Business is actively helping the Tories." Good for him sir! I thought he was a gentleman! You never know – he may even have blue blood.

Yours,

John Beeching

President's reply,

He is at the moment supine behind the bench in the JCR and has been doing nothing all this term. I think this proves your point.

Alan Bennett

(Hilary '59)

Sir,

Here! Ahr bath an ypocahst Guv? Apparently they are very economical to run. You could heat the JCR for a week on three peasants, my old essays, the Alan Reynolds, [a painting] Alan Bennett's old shoes and D Elvice Culver's retchings. Perhaps Mr Morley could illustrate.

Yrs etc,

BW Coulson

Sir,

Mr Coulson should know as well as I do that the fuel value of "retchings" is not merely poor – it is negative. I seem to remember being told of a practical experiment to this end, as a result of which the JCR fire was completely extinguished apparently.

Yrs etc,

David Culver

Sir,

Oh, nothing, just Sir,

Yours sincerely

BW Coulson

P.S. I may be open to correction but the College is very quiet tonight. I hesitate to suggest it, albeit with the most mature reflection, but it is perhaps just a little, Oh. I don't know, perhaps not, well, you know, anyway uninteresting. No, No, No that's what all the cretins say, you know all these bloody trogs, such as Cicero, Isiah (wanna argue Jack?!) Villow and – but I shan't blaspheme,

Yrs again – still sincerely

BW Coulson

(Hilary '57)

A terrible morning Sir, no work here, they're all asleep,
Why don't we all gather up our possessions,

Encluding the old white goat,
And go to the blue mountains of Assam
Where the lily
And the champah never fade.
The tree says,
Enigmatically, oraclewise:
"Dust
in the tearful rallies of Suddipore
will return to dust."

Or you and me?

RJF Moat
(Trinity '58)

Chapter 2
The JCR Books

The JCR Suggestion Books, commonly known among students as the JCR Books, appear to have existed from time immemorial. Their purpose was, as the name implies, to enable undergraduates to voice their suggestions (and complaints) to the President of the Stapeldon Society and thus to the JCR. He was expected to take action. Each book is rather grand, consisting of about 170 foolscap pages, bound in leather with the College crest stamped on the front. It needed to withstand considerable wear and tear, as undergraduates in a drunken state were prone on occasion to throw it about the JCR. Traditionally undergraduates wrote their letters on the right-hand side, usually in ink (generally black, but occasionally blue, green or red) but sometimes with a pencil. The President of the JCR wrote his response on the left hand side, often just 'noted'. Legibility was regularly a problem on the right-hand side.

Completed books were retired to the College archives. Examination of the records shows that in the 20th century prior to 1950 it took a minimum of two years and a maximum of nineteen years to fill a book. However something unusual occurred in the 1950s. Undergraduates no longer stuck to suggestions, but turned to any subject which took their fancy. This encouraged others to respond, and the books fulfilled the role which would now be provided by a chat-room or blog. At the peak of this scriptorial exuberance in 1958, five books were completed. In that year there was also a record run of 25 letters by different writers. It may be no coincidence that 1958 was the year when Zander Wedderburn and subsequently Alan Bennett were the Presidents, since they were prepared to respond with more than "noted".

The other major change was the ability and willingness of a few contributors to draw, as well as to write, in the book. Brian Brindley (1951-1956) regularly drew anything from women's stays to a telephone booth or other architectural fantasies, though always in the gothic style. He was followed by Alan Bennett, Derek Whitelock, and John Morley. This encouraged others such as Malcolm Brown and Bruce Coulson to add drawings to their letters. But, by the beginning of the 1960s drawings disappear and the number of books completed fell back to one or two per year, thus ending the brief golden age of the Exeter College JCR Books.

Most of the letters in this chapter were written in 1957 and 1958. The first was written by the President, Zander Wedderburn, giving statistics on the contents of the book completed in February 1958. This is followed by the Shallcross Supplement of Alan Shallcross, Russell Harty and Alan Bennett. The first two worked at the BBC for much of their careers, as did numerous other graduates from Exeter in the '50s - Ned Sherrin, who was President of the JCR in 1953-4, being one of the best known.

The main entrance to Exeter College is from Turl Street, with a second entrance from Broad Street via Broad Gate – giving rise to John Morley's bizarre drawing of the Broad Gate going neurotic, and his witty drawing of climbing into college via a "Broad".

Most of the letters which have been chosen for inclusion in this book, are printed as they appeared in the JCR Books. Spelling is not every student's forte, and spelling (and grammatical) errors are included, except where they are clearly a mistake or might confuse a reader's understanding.

In fact most of the letters are well-written, regardless of the author's field of study. The main exception related to drunkenness; but almost all such letters had to be excluded as they are largely illegible.

Sir,

Is there any truth in the rumour that MGM are offering £25,000 for the film rights of this book?

Yours sincerely,
JAR de Lange
(Trinity '52)

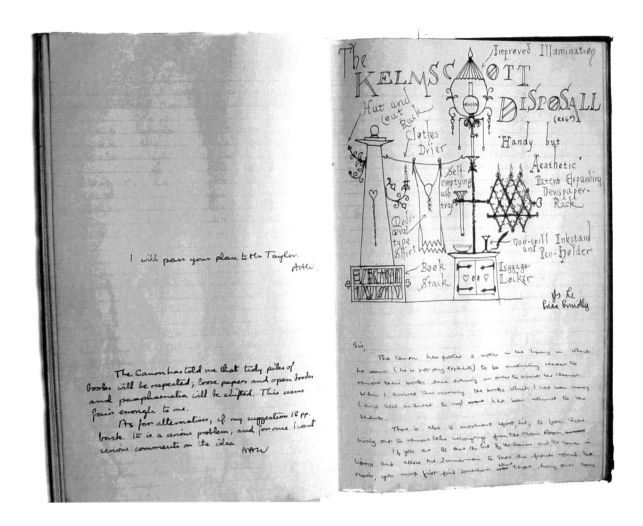

[This sample from 1958 shows two comments by the JCR President, Zander Wedderburn, on the left-hand side, one about the drawing by Brian Brindley on the right-hand side and the other in response to the letter below Brindley's drawing.]

 Craftily as I thought, had I saved up my pennies for a new volume and stealthily, while not unobserved, had I hidden it in the secret knobless drawer; but blow me if this accursed competition in norm-fulfilment hasn't scuppered me.

May I offer you all a motto for this book? It is a creative instrument of which I am proud, and it is good to see how much it is used. If it has a weakness, then perhaps it is to be found in the following.

1) Only 61/307 possible authors contributed to the last volume.

2) 36/61 wrote less than 5 letters.

3) 4 wrote more than 25; 34 was the maximum.

From these statistics I infer:

1) There is a great deal of untapped talent.

2) Some talent is over-tapped.

3) Some is just tapped.

So, before we loose the sluice-gates, let us read Homer

"Always do/be best and better than the rest."

New genuine names are welcome

Old names too, when they are inspired

All vacuity will inter alia be noted.

AAI Wedderburn President
(Hilary '58)

(Hilary '57)

THIS IS THE SPECIAL FREE SHALLCROSS SUPPLEMENT!

Sir,

I have never written in this book before, and, indeed may never write in it again. Would it be possible, however for me to request some guidance in the practice of displaying the exhilarating brand of undergraduate (and graduate) wit, which we are so often privileged to witness?

I am, sir,

Your obedient servant,

Alan Shallcross

Sir,

Surely Mr. Shallcross is secretary of OUDS.

Yrs etc,

Alan Bennett

Ser,

Lais – meme.

HRH JR Harty

Sir,

Illiteracy will get you nowhere.

Yrs,

Alan Shallcross

Sir,

You can talk,

Yrs,

Alan Bennett

Sir,

He certainly can!

Yours,

Russell Harty

(Exoniensis)

(Hilary '57)

[OUDS stands for Oxford University Dramatic Society]

Sir,

This is the first time that I have looked at this book for over twelve months. And five minutes' perusal has been sufficient to convince me that most people here start off with the enormous advantage of having nothing to say and are consequently able to devote all their energies to saying it.

Yours ever,
Christopher RJ Bryant

⸺

Sir,

The JCR windows are disgustingly dirty. Though I am very fond of observing the sun in a Turner glow or an Impressionist haze, I prefer to do this at selected times in the National Gallery and not to have to gaze at the college Secretaries all the time through a glass darkly.

Yrs,
JPH Connell
(at present drinking his wine-dark tea)

⸺

Sir,

.....May I also suggest that we enter into some kind of negotiation with Jesus College about the bells on Sunday morning. Or alternatively, could the JCR provide cotton wool for the people who try and get some sleep between the two fires. Obviously Edgar A Poe once had my room, as he wrote something about the : - "Tintinnabulation of the Bells bells bells bells bells bells bells bells BELLS." Sunday morning is a nightmare instead of being, as it should, a pleasant dream. I am not sure whether it is worse when the two ring together, or when they toss the melody backwards and forwards over my recumbent form. Perhaps unilateral disarmament is the answer.

Yours in distraction,
Philip Heycock
(Michaelmas '60)

⸺

Sir,

....In conclusion, I would like to hope that it was not Mr. Rose who annotated my previous letter, a childish practice I think one can safely leave to those who scribble on lavatory walls.

Yours,
T. Binyon

Sir,

Mr. Binyon's implication that people who annotate letters in this book are on a par with those who "scribble on lavatory walls" is offensive. I scribble on lavatory walls, but I would never, never annotate another gentleman's correspondence.

Yrs,
David Culver
(Michaelmas '57)

Sir,

Would the gentleman who removed my trousers from Mr Roper's room please return them to me as soon as possible since I shall be needing them for the vacation?

Yours etc,
E..G. Pride

Sir,

Pride by name, but not (apparently) pride by nature. When I lose my trousers, I don't blazon it in this book. Nor does Mr A.C.N. Brown (I know this for a fact.)

Yrs etc
Brian Brindley

Sir,

I do not blazon the fact when I lose my trousers, but I do blazon the fact that I have lost my raincoat.

Yrs hopefully,
A.C.N. Brown
(Hilary '55)

PRESENTING JUST COULSON

"William, put that poor cat down at once!" Mr. Coulson's voice rang across the garden. "A'right, a'right", muttered William, moodily pocketing his razor and letting the bleeding creature die in peace. He moved away, trampling over his father's prize leeks. "William! Go and change your shirt at once. It's covered with beer." William glared at his sister Ethel. He'd had enough of this. Picking up a branch he knocked her out with it, dragged the unconscious body across the garden, and buried it in the compost heap. Then, whistling tunelessly, he headed off down the road to call on Ginger Brown, Douglas Graves and Henry Blewitt. They were going to wreck ole Hubert Boulter's birthday party…..

Yrs.

DA Whitelock

Sir,

The birthday party was in full swing. The cream buns and jelly had all been eaten, Violet Elisabeth Spathis had sung "The Swallow's Rising" and Hubert Boulter had been sick.

The Outlaws, in full war-paint (Ethel was at the moment searching vainly and wrathfully for her lipstick and mascara to cover the ravages of an hour covered by decaying vegetation) peered in through the drawing-room window.

"Huh!" commented William scornfully, "call _that_ a party!"

"I dunno," said Ginger doubtfully "there seems to have been n'awful lot to eat."

"I s'pose" said William with withering sarcasm, "I s'pose _you'd_ think people had a good time when they were waitin' to walk the plank, if they had plenty to eat. Crumbs! Look at 'em. Girls 'n' collars 'n' kiss-in- the-ring. Huh!"

And then a soulful look spread over his countenance as he extracted from his pocket, entangled with string and a fluffy toffee bar, Albert his pet hamster. Silently opening the window, he dropped Albert into the party.

Yrs

Malc (Malcolm Brown)
(Hilary '57)

Sir,

Mr Coulson might reflect the next time he wants to fight (or fart) in the JCR that other people are not perhaps as fond of such actions as he appears to be, and that consideration for others, if not self respect, should make him think twice before turning the JCR into an inferior version of the NAAFI.

Yours etc,
JH Morley
(Hilary '58)

Sir,

These beer-darts "dos" make an awful mess of the book. It would be nice if they could be held in a receptacle like this then the "BOOK" would still be nice and clean and legible.

JN Shobbrook
(Hilary '58)

Sir,

I rather fancy that the Broad Gate is open for such a time on most days for all the "numerous reasons why it shouldn't be" to be going neurotic and giving up in disgust. You might name a few just to give people scope to refute them.

Yrs,

RC Hennessy

Sir,

Mr. Hennessy's "fancy" as expressed in the first sentence of his last letter is singularly obscure. I offer the following interpretation of the Broad Gate going neurotic & giving up in disgust. If it does not seem accurate to him, I can only refer him to his original conception.

He washes too often.

Yrs. etc. J.H. Morley.

I'm sorry to quible, but what Mr. Morley has so accurately portrayed is a schizophrenic Broad Gate; and as everyone knows, schizophrenia is a psychosis, not a neurosis.

Yrs in the service of accuracy and Science,

GS Spathis

Sir,

I also am sorry to quibble, but it does have 2 'b's.

Yrs etc,

JH Morley

(Hilary '57)

Sir,

The Intellectual's Lament

A brain
In vain
My exterior
's inferior.

The Charmer's Lament

The drama of me
The house should be packed
But nobody pays
To see me act.

The Musician's Lament

I played with taste
My morals were sham
The d*v*l took notes-
Now look where I am.

The Scholar's Lament

I woo'd the goddess knowledge once.
Sat down to clinch the matter.
My brain is smaller than before
My *rs* is rather fatter

Yrs,
J. Cavanagh
(Trinity '59)

Chapter 3
Brian Brindley

Brian F. Brindley went up to Exeter in 1951 to read Modern History. It was not long before he had taken on two further names, becoming BDFTB, Brian Dominick Frederick Titus Brindley. Perhaps he was influenced by the Senior Tutor in College, who also had five names – John Percy Vivian Dacre Balsdon. In a book of reminiscences written after Brian's death ("Loose Canon" – edited by Damian Thompson), Alan Bennett starts by referring to his extraordinary clutch of names; he doesn't mention that at a later date Brian added a further name, Leo, after Titus.

Brian had won a scholarship to Exeter, although it is clear that studying was relegated below more interesting aspects of College life. He obtained a Third Class degree in 1954, but stayed on to read Law and, perhaps more importantly, to be elected President of the JCR in 1955-56. Alan Bennett describes him in this latter period: "and the carefree days when a whole morning could be whiled away in an armchair in front of the JCR fire, chatting and elaborating some architectural fantasy in the Suggestions Book…"

Although the golden age of the JCR Books is taken roughly as 1954-1959, it is clear that the tenor of the books was beginning to change in the early '50s under the influence of Brian and many of his contemporaries, such as Ned Sherrin, RC Barton, Colin Clowes, GB Dawe, DL Farmer and DA Mitchell. But because Brian stayed on in College, became President, and encouraged the practice of enlivening the books with drawings as well as entertaining letters, he merits a chapter to himself.

Brian left Exeter in 1956, but clearly missed it and was a frequent visitor to the JCR and a continuing contributor to the JCR Books. The chapter finishes with five drawings from this "late period", three of which pay homage to Amelia Jackson, benefactor and wife of former Rector William Jackson.

Sir,

      A large number of sheets of bogpaper this morning are stamped with the excellent phrase 'I like Brindley'. Is one expressing approval or contempt for such a sentiment when one wipes one's rectum with a sheet so marked?

Yrs etc.

C. Clowes

Sir,

Brindley's tastes do now embolden,

For he doth sport a waistcoat golden,

Is this what's known as jeunesse doree?

Do we return to Oscar's glory?

DA Mitchell

Sir,

In answer, tho' it may seem odd o' me,

'Tis not in Coll I practise sodomy.

There's no material – for boys

Need more than pleasant clothes or voice

I look elsewhere for catamites

And out of college spend my nights

But still, no doubt some other bitch'll

Satisfy our curious Mitchell.

BDFT Brindley

Sir,

To answer Brindley's implications:

I seek no "curious" sensations.

All dark desires in them should fail

Who live so near to Reading Gaol.

"—The rest is silence."

DA Mitchell

(Michaelmas '52)

Sir,

Would it be possible for us to have some kind of W.C. in the college bar. Many worthy gentlemen have expressed their annoyance at having to leave their beer unguarded and go off into the wilds in order to P. Perhaps our Mr Brindley could think up some kind of design – gothick? – which would tone in with the bar surroundings. If it is found impossible to so install a W.C., could we just have a big pot placed in a corner for gentlemen's use.

Yours etc.,
V.G. Ogilvie

Sir, Quid pro quo! If gentlemen wish their beer to leave them, they should be prepared to leave their beer. Yrs &c Brian Brindley

P.S. But, just in case, I append a drawing of

Every effort has been made to ensure that both pan and flushing mechanism will fit in with the surroundings of an old-world tavern, and pipage is concealed in the wealth of genuine old oak beams.

Sir,

    Might we ask Mr Brindley to refrain from disrobing in the JCR.

Yours sincerely,
DA Mitchell

Sir, If we may not disrobe *coram publico* in the JCR, may we at least have a

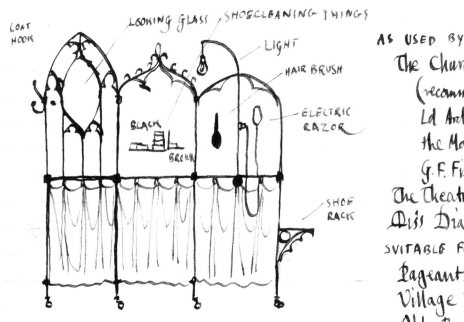

Modestette

REG?

PATENT PORTABL CHANGING-SCREEN

COAT HOOKS — LOOKING GLASS — SHOECLEANING THINGS — LIGHT — HAIR BRUSH — ELECTRIC RAZOR — SHOE RACK — BLACK — BROWN

AS USED BY
The Church
(recommended by H.G. the
Ld Archbp of Canterbury,
the Most Rev. & Rt Hon
G.F. Fisher, DD, Exeter)
The Theatrical Profession
Miss Diana Dors

SUITABLE FOR
Pageants
Village Fetes
Old-Boys' Do's
Army Get-Togethers
Masonic Evenings
&c &c

Mr L. Brian Brindley

STAND (for taking)
BUCK (for passing)
DOE (for raking in)
WHIP (to crack)
POINT (for missing)
NOTICE The following are "too poor" to pay their battels:-
DEAF EAR (for turning)
BAD BLOOD (for causing)
DRAWING-PINS (for putting up notices)
Copy of CREASY'S DECISIVE BATTELS OF HISTORY
The "ORATOR" BURSAR'S COMPANION and Putter-up of Backs.
PATENT APPLIED FOR.
WASTE-PAPER BASKET (for Official letters)
TERMS: Nett Cash; NO CREDIT ALLOWED

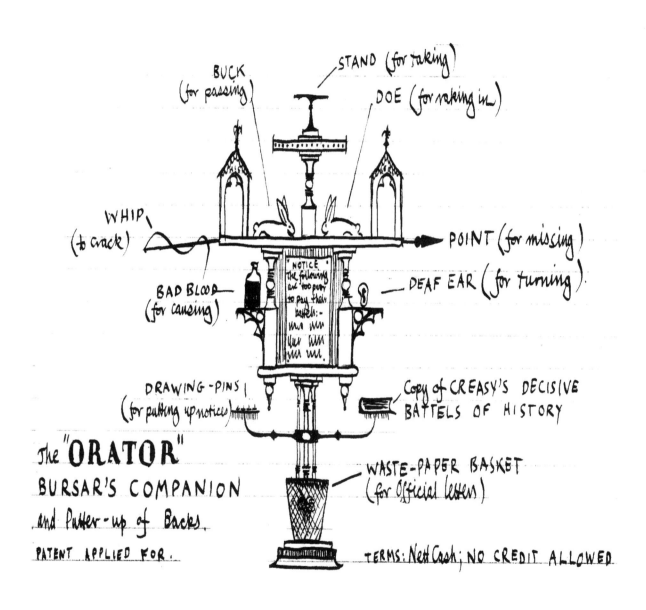

Brian Brindley
(Hilary '55)

merry me in MYSTIC

"*I've never felt so glamorous before,*
My little bulging tummy is no more.
I've sorted out my midriff,
I've flattened out my beam,
I'm uplifted! How my spirits leap and soar.
I've cleared the tummy hurdle,
I've just found the perfect girdle,
And a bra. that makes my bust line look supreme".

Girdle is Model 6096 ; a lovely creation in Peach or White Nylon Voile and Leno elastic net for waist sizes 25″ 36″. Price 84/-.

Bra. is No. C/397 in Peach and White Nylon Taffeta and figured Nylon Voile. Plastic Foam pads in shoulder straps. Sizes 34″ 46″. Price 32/6d.

MYSTIC by ... FITU
BRAS AND GIRDLES

Send card for FREE TAPE MEASURE, leaflet and name of nearest Mystic stockist to FITU, 91, New Bond Street, London, W.I

Sir,

Hereto find appended an extract from a recent 'Woman's Own', included for the benefit of the couple of members of JCR who do not already regularly scrutinize that excellent magazine. In view of the fact that this is only one of the subsidiary attractions – there are lots of letters from 'Worried fourteen-year-old' and 'Materfamilias' – as well as advice on family planning and extermination – oh sir, can't we have a copy here?

Yrs sincerely,
VD Vandervelde
Pp'Fitu' Ltd.

P.S. There is nothing Mystic about my waistline.

(Trinity '55)

gorgeous me in GOTHICK

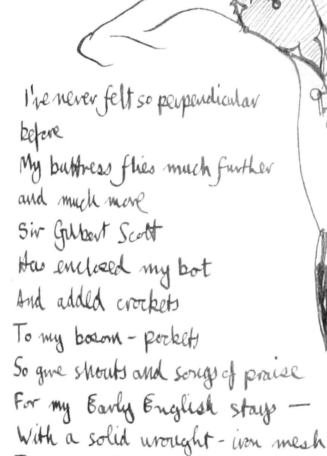

I've never felt so perpendicular
before
My buttress flies much further
and much more
Sir Gilbert Scott
Has enclosed my bot
And added crockets
To my bosom - pockets
So give shouts and songs of praise
For my Early English stays —
With a solid wrought - iron mesh
To cover the sins of my fleche

Yrs,
Brian Brindley
(Trinity '55)

Dear Sir,
    I append a new design for

                    Yrs,
                    Brian Brindley
                    (Hilary ' 55)

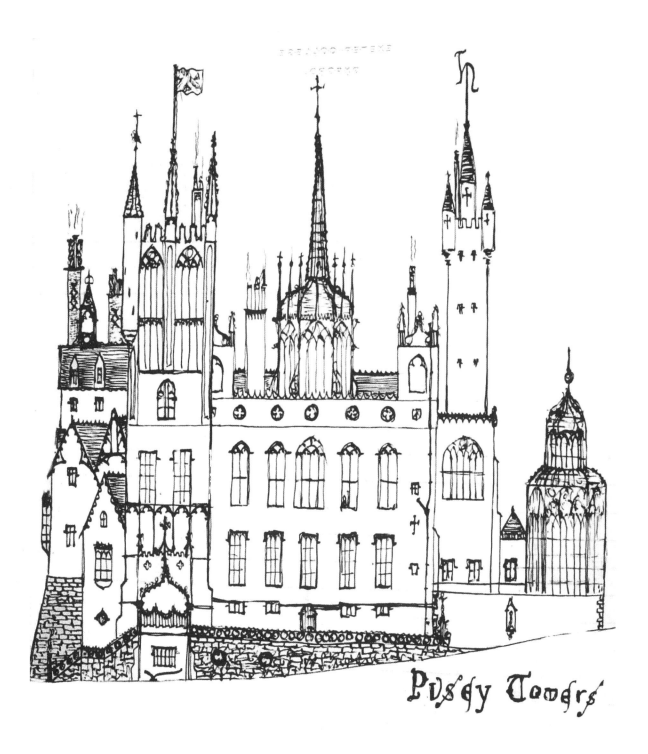

Pusey Towers

[Another architectural fancy by Brian Brindley, President]

(Michaelmas '55)

The Piusseum

You see what I mean, Sir.
As ever,
Brian Brindley

President's reply:
Yes (sighs wearily) I know just what you mean.

Alan Bennett
(Hilary '59)

[Brindley's proposed new building in Oxford in place of that by a Danish architect]

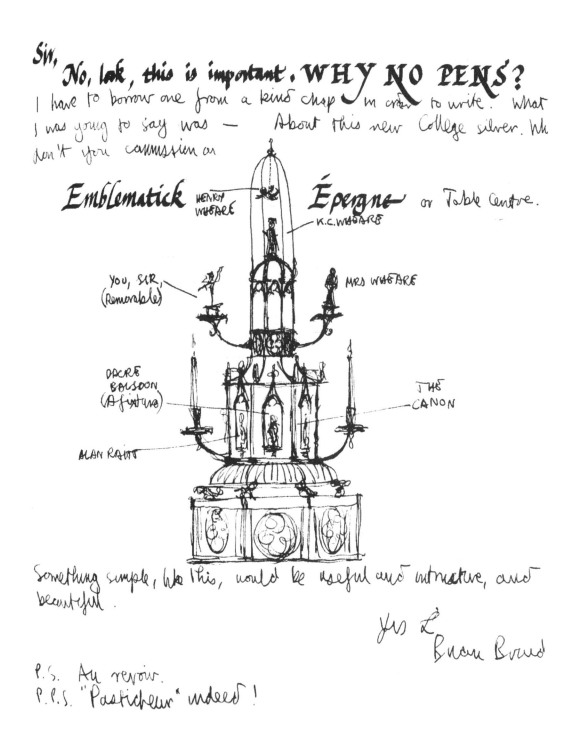

Sir, **No, lok, this is important. WHY NO PENS?**
I have to borrow one from a kind chap in order to write. What I was going to say was — About this new College silver. Wh don't you commission an

Emblematick HENRY WHEARE **Épergne** or Table Centre. K.C.WHEARE

YOU, SIR, (Removable)   MRS WHEARE

DACRE BALSOON (A fixture)   THE CANON

ALAN RAITT

Something simple, like this, would be useful and instructive, and beautiful.

Yrs &
Brian Brind

P.S. Au revoir.
P.P.S. "Pasticheur" indeed!

Sir,

I much prefer old Morley's drawings really. Can't you persuade him to pay us a visit?

John Beeching
(Michaelmas '58)

P.S. Mr Brindley's drawing isn't bad though; I feel William Morris would approve.

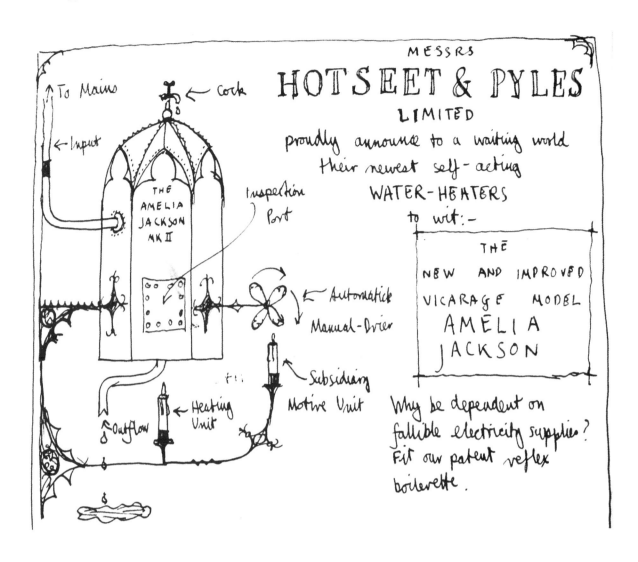

Some Solicited Testimonials: -

"I like my Amelia Jackson" Alan Bennett
"I am hanging on to my Amelia Jackson." R. Ben Jones
"A fair dinkum article." R.C. Wheare
"Why should you believe what I say." Mrs Wheare
"Very cold on the hole this morning." E.A. Barber
"Fantastic" Dacre Balsdon
Fit our fitments and be satisfied. As supplied exclusively to the Vatican, the Rector's lodgings, Two Trees Hernes Road, the Star Chamber, the Deanery Canterbury and the haunts of the Nobility, Clergy and Gentry.

Brian Brindley
(Michaelmas ' 57)

[Two Trees Hernes Road was the private address of then Rector Eric Arthur Barber.]

Sir,

Who says (Mr Meakin 3pp back) that Corset Advertisements have anything to do with sex? There has recently come into my possession the following:

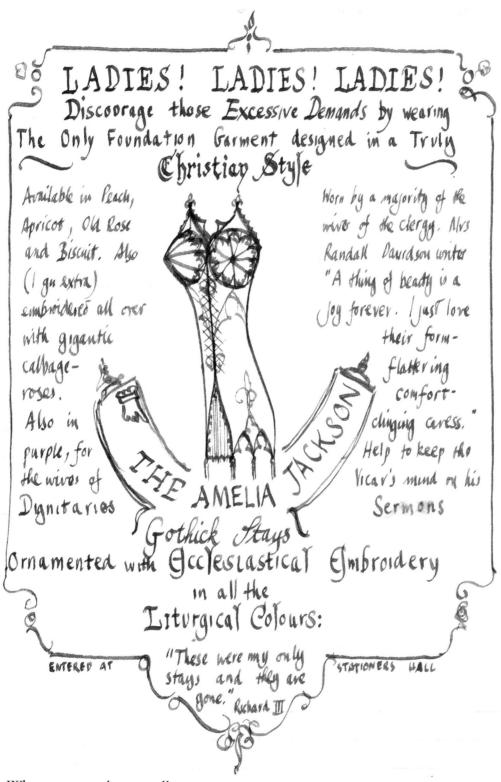

LADIES! LADIES! LADIES!
Discourage those Excessive Demands by wearing
The Only Foundation Garment designed in a Truly
Christian Style

Available in Peach, Apricot, Old Rose and Biscuit. Also (1 gn extra) embroidered all over with gigantic cabbage-roses. Also in purple, for the wives of Dignitaries

Worn by a majority of the wives of the clergy. Mrs Randall Davidson writes "A thing of beauty is a joy forever. I just love their form-flattering comfort-clinging caress." Help to keep the Vicar's mind off his Sermons

THE AMELIA JACKSON

Gothick Stays
Ornamented with Ecclesiastical Embroidery
in all the Liturgical Colours:

"These were my only stays and they are gone." Richard III

ENTERED AT   STATIONERS HALL

What an example to us all.

Yrs,

Brian Brindley
(Michaelmas '59)

Sir,

Cleanliness is, I grant you, next to godliness, but there are times when it can be bought at too high a price. The telephone arrangements consequent upon the recent sanitary installations are (not to put too fine a point upon it) A DISGRACE. May I suggest the installation of a new and ornamental KIOSK; it could be placed conspicuously in the middle of the front Quad, where it would not only enhance the decorative appeal of the old coll: but also ensure a salutary measure of publicity for those who are constantly telephoning their bookmakers, mistresses, probation officers etc. Something not uncomely can be bought commercially such as

The Amelia Jackson
Patent Prefabrickated Cast-Iron and
Glass Electrick Telephone Booth
"A thing of Beauty is a Joy for ever"

Yrs etc
Brian Brindley

President's reply
Bravo! We were about due for a spot of the teutonic high gothic.

John Moat
(Michaelmas '59)

Chapter 4
College Life

Exeter College was one of the smaller colleges in the 1950s, with around 300 undergraduates, of whom about 100 lived in College, mostly freshmen (1st year undergraduates). The remainder lived in "digs" (a rented room or flat) in Oxford. It wasn't a grand college, like Christ Church or Magdalen; but it had a reputation as a friendly college, with life visibly centred on the JCR and the College bar in the Front Quad.

There are two letters from Mr. Field Evans (1952) and Mr Wells-Furby (1957) critical of freshmen. Both expected first-year students to be seen but not heard. This was not a widely-held belief.

The College rooms all had two doors. The outer door, the "oak", when closed ("sported") could only be opened from the inside. The theory was that an oak would be sported when the occupant was working and did not want to be disturbed. The problem arose when two undergraduates shared a suite of rooms (a common living-room and a small bedroom each), and one of them sported the oak in order to entertain a girl-friend. There are 3 amusing letters on the subject, plus Alan Bennett's response as JCR President of how he handled the situation in his first year. However the College decided to remove the oaks in 1958, which led to a storm of protest. The Senior Tutor, JPV Dacre Balsdon, wasn't too pleased either, having just published a book on Oxford Life, described by a reviewer as seen "not so much through rose-coloured spectacles as tinted contact lenses."

The hours during which an undergraduate could entertain a female guest in College were from 2pm-4pm in 1955, but were extended to 7:30pm a year or so later. This was extremely frustrating, and led to regular letters of complaint. Several students often misjudged the time, and would thus have to ask a neighbour to distract the attention of the College porter while he hustled his girl-friend out through the lodge in order to avoid a fine. Of course in the 1950s there were about five times as many male as female undergraduates at Oxford, who resided some distance away and who tended to be fairly choosy in their pick of potential suitors. As a result, there was much boasting in the JCR about conquests, real or imaginary, with the advantage that extravagant claims could hardly ever be proved, except perhaps in the case of one undergraduate with a room in Palmer's Tower, to which Oxford High School girls in straw boaters could be seen making their way on summer afternoons. Charitable explanations that only afternoon tea was involved were weakened on one occasion by the sight of an irate mother trying to force open the gentleman's oak.

For those with a room in College, the problem could be getting in, as the gate was locked at midnight. Those who stayed out beyond the witching hour without permission were also fined. There were two alternative routes in – either climbing over the College wall with the help of a drainpipe, or through a window onto Broad Street whose lock had been tampered with.

Sir,

I believe it was Lincoln College JCR which obtained concessions from their SCR [Senior Common Room] by a certain agitation. I believe the time by which ladies had to leave college was extended to 10:30pm, and gate fines were abolished. The latter concession I think is not required, for the cost of keeping the Porters on duty late at night is partly borne by those responsible. But the early hour that ladies must leave college is an anomaly. The SCR treats us as rational , fairly mature people in many things, but as libidinous schoolchildren in this respect. I think the JCR might welcome an extension of the hours for ladies in college; personally I do not benefit, but feel the rule is antiquated and useless.

Yours sincerely,
Michael Barton, DA Whitelock

President's reply:

I am told by the Sub Rector that any gentleman who wishes to entertain a lady in his room after 7:30 only has to get permission from him to do so. He also tells me that he does not remember having refused permission on many occasions. He does not feel there is any real hardship.

SK Guram

Sir,

If Mr. Roper had to get permission to dispense coffee after midnight, we might never get any! Similarly, if one has to take deliberate and premeditated action to be able to entertain young ladies after 7:30, there is a distinct probability that they never get any either.

Yrs etc,
Malcolm Brown

Sir,

That's the point: I know the Sub-Rector gives permission easily, but the fact remains we should not have to make a formal application up to a reasonable hour, which 7:30 certainly is not. It is galling not to be allowed to take ladies into one's home for almost half the year unless one has planned it by 2 o'clock. Surely the Sub-Rector will see the reasonableness of this.

Yours sincerely
Michael T Barton

Sir,

...... It is not every day I find myself on all fours with Messers Barton, Whitelock and Farmer, but on this question I am (as always) their wholehearted supporter. Both when I lived in college, and when I moved out, this foolish rule vexed me – your predecessor called me "an old fraud" if you please. Why should people have to get permission, however easily it may be done. May I suggest that, from tomorrow (or say next Monday) there should be a crowd of people at the Sub-Rector's At Home time EVERY DAY, asking (and according to you, obtaining) leave to entertain one lady each in their rooms until, say, 10 o'clock. After a week, we should have no more of this nonsense.

Yrs, cutting his own throat,
Brian Brindley
(Trinity '55)

Dear Sir,

I suppose everyone who knows J (Jean-Jacques) Ashw**th has realised that, since the arrival of the scholarly M. M*ll*t, he has strained to acquire 'le personalite François'. He can smoke French cigarettes – OK. He can shake hands with everyone all the time (even Carruthers) – OK. BUT (and this is a big BUT) to preserve the present, quite reasonable state of Anglo-French relations, please don't let him say anything more French than ' Bon jour' --BECAUSE (and this is the point), when he was in lunch today, he was (of course) sitting next to the venerable M. M*ll*t, and, in course of conversation said, It's a 'nom-de-plume' and subsequently the chat went as follows.

Jacques "A what?"

John   "Nom-de-plume"

Jacques "A what?"

John   "Nom de plume"

Jacques ditto

John   ditto

Jacques ditto

John   ditto

And ditto and ditto until it seemed the year dotto, had not John said, "It means another name, an assumed one." To which Jacques replied, "Oh!---I'm sorry, I thought you were speaking English."

So, Please Pres., exhort him to use only London, the language he speaks best, or else these entente cordiales and things will be no good, will they?

JN Shobbrook

(Hilary ' 58)

Sir,

I would be glad if you would remonstrate with Mr. Dorling on his outrageous familiarity. This crass and ignorant oaf has the temerity to refer to me by my Christian name – we have not been introduced. I hope we never shall be.

This type of ill-mannered behaviour is representative of this year's freshmen.

Yours,

John Field Evans

President's reply:

It is the custom to refer to gentlemen as Mr so-and-so.

ER Larsen

Dear Sir,

Again Mr. John Field Evans' impudence astounds me. Not having contributed one jot to the academic standing of the college, not one tittle to its sporting reputation and not one iota to its social activities, he has the audacity to jibe at the freshman – that fine body of men, whose energy, friendliness, academic distinction the senior men so much admire. No one will be sorry to see the Evil Man depart to the sordid foothills of Wales next summer, I'm sure. And I hope he takes Mr. Dorling with him.

Yours sincerely,

CJ Sheward (Michaelmas '52)

Sir,

Does Mr. Wells-Furby have to assert the fact that he is not one of that common class, the "bourgeois", by throwing cups, spoons and coffee on people on the lawn after dinner? We are all acquainted with Mr Wells-Furby's dialectical and verbal capacities, but I hesitate to add to this thrilling list the ability to prove Newton's laws of mechanics as applied to projectiles

Yours sincerely,

P Kuczynski

President's reply:

If you had asked him, he would have told you that it was the inalienable right of fourth year men to throw cups, spoons and coffee at other fourth year men without comment from insolent freshmen. This of course is tripe, but you could never convince him of this.

NR Graves

Sir,

Let the freshmen mind their P's and Q's and allow more senior members of this college to decay according to their own lights.

Yrs etc,

HE Wells-Furby

Sir,

Much as I appreciate Komrad Kuczynski's taking up cudgels (in lieu of coffee cups et. al.) on my behalf, I think that after 4 years of Mr. Wells-Furby's company I am quite capable of defending myself against him unaided. I hope therefore, that in future, he (the first mentioned) will mind his own "bloody" business.

Yrs etc,

JG Stamper

Sir,

Mr. Wells-Furby is renowned for the interest he takes in seeing that Freshmen measure up to the standard he requires of them, and anyway I hope we have now passed the Public School stage, where Juniors must take care not to be 'bumptious' to Seniors.

Yours,

JG Speirs

Sir,

I am not interested in freshmen.

Yrs etc,

HE Wells-Furby

Sir,

After 4 years Mr Wells-Furby MUST be getting bored with Freshmen.

Yrs,

RW Clements

Sir,

    We, the undersigned freshmen, regret Mr. Wells-Furby's lack of interest in us, which surprises us no end, and wish to record that for our part, we think he's rather nice.

DE Culver

(Trinity '57)

━ ~

Sir,

    How unchapish can a chap get? Mr. Whitelock, with no more warning than a muttered 'wheels within wheels', has ensconced himself and, knowing Mr Whitelock, some disreputable, (but still to be pitied), wench in my room, and sported my oak on me. Wheels no doubt grind first, (though not, as we know, as fine as Mr. Whitelock) but what the blazes does he mean? Poor scientist that I am, I have an Essay to do. This sort of thing would never be tolerated in the laboratories, 'a-frizzling for neuromancy, indeed!' If this was a right thinking world, Mr. Whitelock would be a castrato for irreverence. And in front of my hamster, too.

G.S. Spathis

(Hilary '57)

Sir,

    I, as the freshest of freshmen, have spent a miserable evening sitting in an armchair in this room, gazing with passionate desire at the lighted window which I can see across the quad. Ensconced behind the tightly-drawn curtains are my room-mate and an attractive specimen of femininity.

    Ever since the bar shut, I have by the dictates of common decency been kept from my whisky-bottle.

    It seems quite clear to the meanest intelligence, sir, that the case against room-sharing is proved many times o'er.

    Could something be done?

Yours in anticipation,

DA Askew

Sir,

    Mr. Askew should either:

1) Bring his whisky into the JCR or

2) Get a woman and get there (his room) first.

Yrs sincerely,

Michael Phospos

President's reply:

    There can be few people left in the college who can recall my own room-mate, a Mr. Whitelock. Your predicament precisely paralleled my own in my first year – hem-hem – only I was shut out at least three times a week 3:30pm – 7:30 pm.

    There are remedies:

    I once arranged for certain members of the Oxford University Orchestra to leave their instruments in the room when a session was due to take place. They then called for the instruments individually at intervals of 10 minutes throughout the said session.

Alan Bennett

(Michaelmas '58)

Sir,

A Happy New Year to you – (and all our readers!) Where are the oaks from staircase 8? Their removal is a serious denial of human rights. It becomes a very grave matter when it is impossible to enjoy the privacy of one's room.

Let this be your resolution for 1958
GET US BACK OUR OAKS.

Yours,
Robin M. Beechey

President's reply:

The official explanation is:-

1 They are never used
2 They collect dust
3 They would have to be painted
4 There is a shortage of firewood

If individuals affected pester the authorities (the Bursar) with vigorous denials of 1 (above), further inroads on our privacy will be forestalled, and some unchopped oak may be restored.

AAI Wedderburn

Sir,

Regretful though I am to enter the lists so early, I really think someone ought to speak to the Bursar. Does JPVD Oxford Life B [Dacre Balsdon] know about this. It makes several sections of his book out of date. I remember my oak was very much used in my first year – not by me, of course, but by Whitelock. Also has the Bursar removed his own oak? Besides, the whole college collects dust. If you started knocking down and burning everything that collected dust (Bedson periodically suggests this) what would you do with the Ford foundation money.

Yrs,
Alan Bennett

Sir,

Dacre's answer when told about the oaks was, "Make a fuss, man. Make a fuss; make a fuss. Or else get them to give you keys."

GIVE US BACK OUR OAKS OR KEYS

Yours sincerely,
M Seakins
(Hilary '58)

Sir,

If the orchid of seriousness may obtrude itself among the cabbages of frivolity… I would like to bring to your attention, Sir, a rather saddening experience of mine. Going upstairs to Mr. Bedson's attic last night I was intrigued by sounds of sawing and chopping coming through the door. "Carpentry?" I murmured to myself. "Fretwork?" – gladly supposing that Mr. Bedson had hit upon this innocent hobby to take his mind off the werewolf complex. But, Sir, what a spectacle met my gaze when I opened the door! The room was simply stacked with the mutilated corpses of members of the college.

There was Parkers, soldierly to the last, side by side with the scarcely bleeding remains of Mr. Graves. There was Mr. Sissons, a libidinous leer frozen on his lifeless lineaments: There, too, was Mr. Wedderburn, a porage spoon clutched in his hand: the putrefying cadaver of Mr. Joy grinned from a corner. Mr. Bedson in a butcher's apron, was busy with a cleaver on what had once been Mr. Short. "Adrian! Adrian!" I cried, not a little upset by all this. "What are you doing?" "He! He! He!" returned the other, "making pies."

Yrs,

DA Whitelock

P.S. I believe he thinks he is Titus Andronicus now.

Sir,

We feel sure that all readers of this book will appreciate Mr Whitelock's amusing account of his visit to the Stapledon Bakery. The interesting pies which he mentions left the ovens this morning; the more ghoulish members of the College, who had been awaiting the event, had first go and unanimous approval was expressed. The pies are now generally available, some with more gravy, some with less, but all guaranteed not to contain any of Mr Bennett's hairs. We do not actually remember Mr Bennett being one of the company last night, anyway. The most likely explanation is that he was there disguised as a corpse, collecting the victim's signatures for the abolition of capital punishment, a cause dear to their hearts. However we can state without fear of contradiction that all the chaps voted it a jolly good show.

Anticipating your esteemed enquiries, we are,

Yours faithfully,

The Stapledon Pie Co. Ltd.

(Hilary '56)

Brian Brindley, President
(Hilary '56)

Sir,

Mr.Beechey told me today that I ought to be annoyed because he had only been fined one half-crown (party-rate, hockey team) for climbing in after 12, while I was fined one half-bar for climbing in before 12. Well, I'm not annoyed, and good luck to Beechey.

Mr. Pritchard has insinuated that I climbed in before 12 to save 6 pence. I resent this. At the time I had not worked out specific reasons for the action, but in effect they were

1) To avoid walking round into the Turl from BNC [Brasenose College]
2) To keep in practice
3) To save 6 pence....
4) To avoid the stroppy porter who still knows hardly any of our names.

So justified, I hope, I retire to bed as:

Yours sincerely,

Michael Seakins

Sir,

This is the second time of asking (the last time was in the middle of last term). Will you get someone to fix the drainpipe outside Mr Wordsworth's bedroom? It is getting quite dangerous to climb in over the wall. Also some fiend takes delight in placing damn great rocks in the flowerbed underneath.

Yours sincerely.

M Seakins

(Hilary '58)

Sir,

Maybe you've never been at a party gatecrashed by David Cecil and W.H. Auden. Even if you have, please don't be tempted to enter college via the Clarendon Bldgs. and the wall by the Divinity Schools etc.. There I was, having effected an entrance at 0020 and on a ladder against that particular wall when a door of the Museum of Science opens and emerges a man and a bloodhound. Even a reputable hurdler would gulp before clearing that 3'6" iron-speared fencing, leap 10' down over Barltrop's dustbins where there was still a vicious dog at his heels. The point is this: it may be degrading to climb through a window on the broad, but do so nonetheless.

Yours sincerely,
M Seakins

(Trinity '58)

Sir,

As I passed the end section of LMH [Lady Margaret Hall] at 10:25 this evening a girl was visible on the second floor putting on lipstick using a saucepan as a mirror. At 10:37 the same girl was in the same position vying for mirror-saucepan space with another one combing her hair. Moral – if you are joining in the punt scheme next term invest another 5 pence in a Woolworth's mirror if you're stopping at LMH so as to obtain a presentable female.

Yours sincerely,

M Seakins

Sir,

LMH must have some very shiny bottoms, unlike those in Sandfield Rd, most of which are blackened with constant heat.

Luv,

Malc. XXX

[Malcolm Brown]

(Hilary '58)

Sir,

Two pieces of gossip:

1) Nigel Graves: "I would never wear a kilt, but I have very nice legs."

2) Mr Ashworth went to the Sub-Rector to get permission for a party on St Valentine's Day. On telling him the party was for ONE, the Sub-Rector tore up the chit, and said firmly, "Mr Ashworth, a party does not consist of one."

Hey, ho,

JG Speirs

(Hilary '58)

Sir,

Did you ever have one of those evenings which start off when you tell your bird that you'd like to see Arnold Wesker and she gives you the old comeback of 'Who does he play for?', and she rather fancies Gigi? Whereupon you manage to sway the issue only by the promise of two hot dogs at the end of the evening (one with, one without). And then there's the old trick where you'd discovered that you had only about one eighth of an inch of after-shave lotion, so you'd decided on a scheme of spreading it on only one side of your face. But the usherette cocks everything up and you find yourself on your wrong side. So, not wanting to be too explicit, you motion to your bird with your arms that you'd like to change places, but she's a bit thick and just crosses her legs. So you end up with your Old Spice drifting over a bloke who in the dark bears a marked resemblance to T. Fitzgerald, but in the interval turns out to be wearing cavalry twill. Then, to cap it all, as it were, your bird whiffs your breath and says it must have been Crawfords, which of course it was. The only consolation at all was that the hot dog man had been arrested again (unlicensed pickle), so you saved yourself a bob or two. But otherwise very bad news.

Yrs,

Michael Schofield

(Michaelmas '60)

Dear Sir,

Herewith a draft of letter which I am intending to write to the Express (Daily or Sunday)….

I am a student at an Oxford college which shall be nameless. Our bar is opposite Jesus College and the other day, in an excess of fervour, Saturday evening to be precise, we were singing God Save the Queen, God Bless her darlin' little bum, and our Sub-Rector said, "I do not like that song, you will please stop singing it."

Sir, this is worthy of investigation, I feel; is our Sub-Rector a Red? I mean we luv our Queen.

David Culver

President's reply:
Extract from the Sunday Express, Sunday, November 2nd

"A nasty incident occurred in Oxford last week-end. A crowd of healthy, happy young lads thought they'd like to pay a loyal tribute to their Queen in their college bar. As one man they stood up and toasted Her Majesty and sang with their lusty and healthy young voices, the National Anthem. What more fitting? What more proper?

And what happened? How was this spontaneous expression of loyalty and enthusiasm greeted?

They were told to stop it. Told to shut up.

And why? Because they were making too much noise. They offended the ears of a passing don, on his way to a concert. A concert. And not even an orchestral concert. A concert of viols.

And who is this man who stands in the way of our boys expressing their loyalty and enthusiasm? He is Dr. Alan Wagstaff Raitt, B.A., the deputy Rector of Exeter College. Has he done his National Service? Has he fought in Cyprus? Has he guarded helpless British mothers in the streets of Famagusta? No. What does he do for a living? He teaches literature. French literature. I suppose English literature isn't good enough for him? These are the men to whom we commit the future of our lads – disloyal perverts and weaklings. And who pays for it all? Who puts the money into Mr. A.W. Raitts pocket? You do. The housewife, the docker, the policeman. All of us. Why haven't we got more sense?

Alan Bennett
(Michaelmas '58)

Sir,

When are we going to be allowed to play bowls? What the hell is this institution – a worm preservation society? Let them have good healthy sport dodging the 'woods'. And I shall dislike any restriction on playing time too – the idea that 'gentlemen should allow grass to grow in the mornings' smacks rather.

Not that I want to play bowls anyway really. It's purely the fact that I am not allowed to is my grouse. After all, the summer – sorry Trinners – term is the bowls season; after which I close.

Yours,

M.J. Moffatt (Punch Extraordinary)

Sir,

I have not had the pleasure of being introduced to Mr. Moffatt. There are some conclusions I draw about him from his latest letter.

1. He asks when we are going to be able to play bowls. This is clearly stated in a notice on the subject. First indictment – ignorance.

2. He automatically connects worms and bowls – playing. In Dylan Thomas the worm is the frequently reiterated symbol of decay. Second indictment – pessimism.

3. He thinks worms enjoy dodging bowls. No doubt he claims that foxes enjoy the hunt. Third indictment – brutality.

4. Though he does not want to play bowls, he does not like restrictions on it. The Whitehead complex or the freedom of society to choose the worse course. Alternatively he wants (fourth indictment) anarchy.

5. He needs to grumble – fifth indictment – discontent.

However on looking back over his previous letters, I see they deal with Urinals, Soliciting, Eavesdropping, the Christmas Spirit, the Romantic Spirit and not unsurprisingly injections. Elsewhere he talks (impertinently) of <u>tone-raising</u>.

Yours,
JPH Connell, Arbiter Elegantiae

Sir,

I caught Mr Connell surreptitiously reading over his last letter but one, [above] with a smug, satisfied smile on his face. The said letter had been written at least 24 hours before; so one wonders how often Mr Connell had read over this said letter in the intervening period. I cannot see any corrections added to it so presumably he is quite happy about the rotten fruit of his labours.

Yrs,
JG Speirs

4 times in fact.

JPH Connell

President's response

He sometimes comes up to my room and spends a happy, time-beguiling hour browsing through his "bijoux" in the back numbers.

John Moat
(Trinity '60)

Sir,

I feel I must let you take advantage of a useful railway service I investigated this afternoon (and evening) between Paddington and Oxford. It really cheered me up after a tiring day of interviews with Shell.

I was fortunate in being directed onto the Cathedrals Express by an inspired Paddington ticket collector instead of the rather uninteresting 5:15 Oxford train. A minor disadvantage of this express seemed to be that its first stop was Newport (Mon) but this was more than balanced by the excellent connections available for completing the journey. After only 20 mins wait a train arrived for Swindon (half an hour wait), then on to Didcot. Here, I broke the inevitable half hour wait with a very good-news bowl of oxtail soup price nine pence (c.f. coffee ten pence).

The last train was slightly late, I must admit, arriving in Oxford at 10:35.

Overall, then, a very commendable time of five and a half hours with an average speed well over 10 mph (c.f. goods traffic 3mph) – probable faster than one could sprint it.

B.R. waiter – "Educoishonul anyway."

Yours in anguish
JM Ketteringham

President's reply (comes from one of Bennett's sermons):
An employee of the Railway Company hailed me, and said,
"Hi Jack, where do you think you're going?" That at any rate was the gist of what he said.

Roger Thorn
(Michaelmas '60)

Dear Sir,

(Only sleep is sour)
why let them walk
on Sunday afternoons
in high heels:
pernickety
and noisily neat
like coins dropped
in my small box
(sandal wood scented)
of savings.
Keep'em out, old boy, keep 'em out.

Yours after lunch,
RJF Moat
(Hilary '58)

Chapter 5
Alan Bennett

Alan Bennett came up to Exeter in 1954 to read Modern History, and obtained a First Class degree in 1957. Fortunately he decided to stay up to obtain a further degree, and it was in this period that he started to develop that personal voice which shines through all of his work – in the theatre, on the radio, on television, and in his books and diaries. He was a regular contributor to the JCR Books – in 1957-58 there is an amusing contribution when he strayed across to write on the President's side and was sharply told by the then President, Zander Wedderburn, to return to the right-hand side. In the summer of 1958 he himself was elected President for the year 1958-59, thus returning legitimately to the left-hand pages of the book, where he wrote more and even more entertainingly than his eminent predecessors. Writing "noted" as his response to a letter was definitely a last resort.

In a recent contribution to the book 'Loose Canon' about one of his Presidential predecessors, Brian Brindley, Alan mentions that he felt intimidated by him. By 1958 this would have seemed odd to his contemporaries, because he was himself overwhelmingly the dominant person in the JCR. In 1957-58 he had been elected Chairman of the Kitchen Committee, which met the Bursar and the Chef about twice a term. It was an interesting year. Alan took the job seriously, which the Bursar and Chef were clearly not used to. It didn't help that Alan entertained a huge dislike of the Chef's cat, Carruthers (see Chapter 11), on the grounds of hygiene (marked lack of). It was rumoured that after each meeting the Chef handed in his notice, which the Bursar spent the next week persuading him to withdraw. No doubt it was somewhat less frequent!

In Chapter 2 there is an explanation of the role of the Stapeldon Society, of which all undergraduates were members. As President of the JCR and Chairman of the Society, Alan realised his gift for capturing the attention of an audience and keeping it hugely entertained. It was the practice to follow the last meeting of the Stapeldon Society before Christmas with a "Smoker", at which members of the college endeavoured to entertain their colleagues. There is no doubt that at the Smoker of 1958 not all of those present will recall Ken Rose's recitation of "Eskimo Nell" or the take-off by John Barraclough and John Speirs of the College Operatic Society's recent production of "Lord Bateman" entitled "Master Bateman". However all those who were present will remember Alan's first public performances of his sermon and his version of the Queen's Christmas Broadcast which led in time to his contribution to "Beyond the Fringe" in Edinburgh, London and New York.

In this chapter there are some splendid drawings of Alan, a few by himself (he almost always drew himself) but mainly by that artistic genius, John Morley (see Chapter 8). There are also numerous letters and comments by Alan, as President, about the letters of other contributors. However his contribution was so pervasive that other letters by him appear throughout this book.

Sir,

   A preview of three stalwarts of the Aesthetes' XI, the Poetic Dribblers, who meet the Hockey team next Thursday at the Exeter College Ground.

                    Yrs,
                         Eamonn Whitelock
                         [alias DA Whitelock]

ALAN "CANNONBALL" BENNETT, DYNAMIC,
GOAL-WHAMMING CENTRE FORWARD FROM LEEDS.
DESCRIBING HIMSELF AS A "COMMON, WORKING
CHAP" SANITARY ENGINEER BENNETT CLAIMS
"THEM BLOKES WON'T KNOW WHAT HIT 'EM"

[Alan "Cannonball" Bennett, dynamic, goal-whamming centre forward from Leeds.]
[Describing himself as a "common, working chap" sanitary engineer, Bennett claims "them blokes won't know what hit 'em."]

[Tough, quick-kicking A.J. "Bruiser" Bedson, one of the most destructive full backs in the business.]

["Dames?" grunts Bedson.]

["Gimme railway engines any day."]

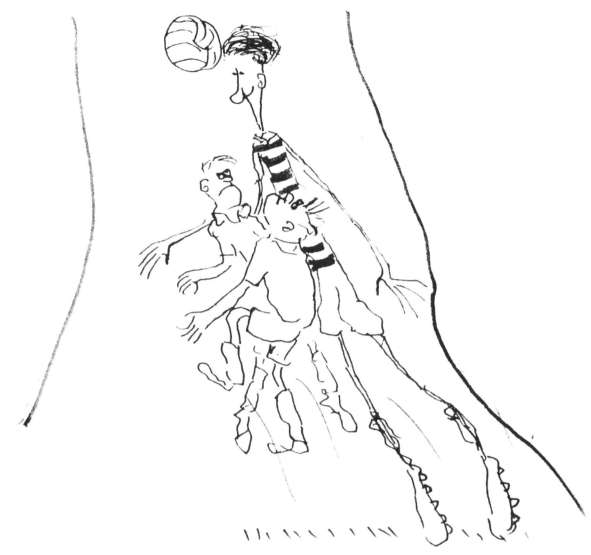

NIJE "NETTEM" GRAVES, COLCHESTER
THUNDERBOLT. A TOWER OF STRENGTH ON THE
WING. HAPPILY MARRIED, WITH 8 CHILDREN, NIJE WORKS
AS AN APPRENTICE SCREW FITTER.
" WE'LL HAMMER 'EM " GRINS NIJE.

(Hilary '56)

[Nije "Nettem" Graves, Colchester thunderbolt. A tower of strength on the wing. Happily married, with 8 children, Nije works as an apprentice screw fitter.]
["We'll hammer 'em" grins Nije.]

Partidge says I have to
apologise to everyone for being
so rude to everyone, so
I do(but not to J.H. M*rley; J. B*ulter; N.R. Gr*ves;
H. W*lls F*rby; P.M. Th*mas; D.E Garr*od; P.P K**cz*z*—
V*s** k* i; D.A Wh*bl*ck; B d'E.F.W. And*rson;
R.S.W. N.C.H Cl*m*nts; N*gel F**xell; J.G Sp*us
J G Sp*eo; J. G Sp*eo; J.G Sp*us; J.G Sp*rs;
St*n Haigh ⁵; The Chef.   His cat   ⎫did you
              The chef.   His cat   ⎬smell the
              The chef   His cat   ⎭spoons
              The chef.   His cat   yauic
              The chef   His cat
              The Chef   His cat.

Alan Bennett
(Hilary '57)

Sir,

Mr. Bennett [thank God] is back, sprightly and gay as ever.

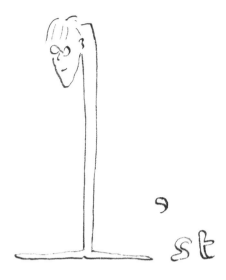

But his shape seems to have changed.
Yours etc.
J.H Morley.

Sir,

Mr. Bennett ought to be careful. The 3 Y fronts app be running away with him.

Carruthers [cynical as usual]
Yrs. etc J.H Morley.

(Michaelmas '57)

Sir,

Mr. Bennett appears to be adopting a singularly mournful costume nowadays.

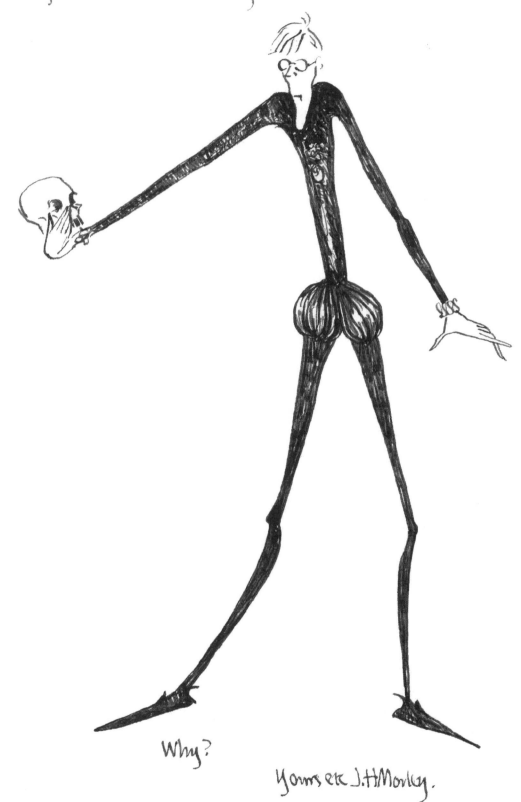

Why?

Yours etc J.H.Morley.

(Michaelmas '57)

Sir,
The National Press has recently been commenting on Mr. Alan Bennett and a venture known as the "Bucket of Blood."

I would like to know if, as I suspect, Mr. Graves has been giving him any assistance in this.
Yours etc JHMorley.

(Michaelmas '57)

Sir,

Could we have this arm by the fire mended please. It used to be the other end that was loose; now it's this one.

Morley is just about to start one of his metaphysical squash games with Partridge, Partridge having thrown the metaphysical ball in the air for service with 'Truth is simple.' Morley volleyed with a loud "Oh!" Duce. (Binners says no Duce in squash.)

Yrs etc,
A Bennett

Nor so he says do you spell it comme ca but Deuce. Or Duse?

Sir,

Mr Bennett's conceptions seem slightly mixed. Neither Eleanora nor Benito have anything to do with squash.

Yrs,
TJ Binyon

Sir,

Actually Mr Binyon gave me 8 and a half pence to write my letter with the deliberate mistakes so that he could put his slick little witty remarks in. I have put 8 pence in the Barnardos box. I gave him a half penny back. I had borrowed his pen, you see.

Yrs,
A Bennett

Sir,

I haven't had eight and a half pence for years.

Yours,
TJ Binyon

Sir,

What a cosy little altercation is the above! Note that even their respective handwriting is growing rapidly indistinguishable. I believe that Bennett-Binyon, together form a complete personality – the shy, quivering-ears, lissom Bennett, and the square, sensible, squared-toed Binyon.

Yrs etc,
JH Morley
(Hilary '58)

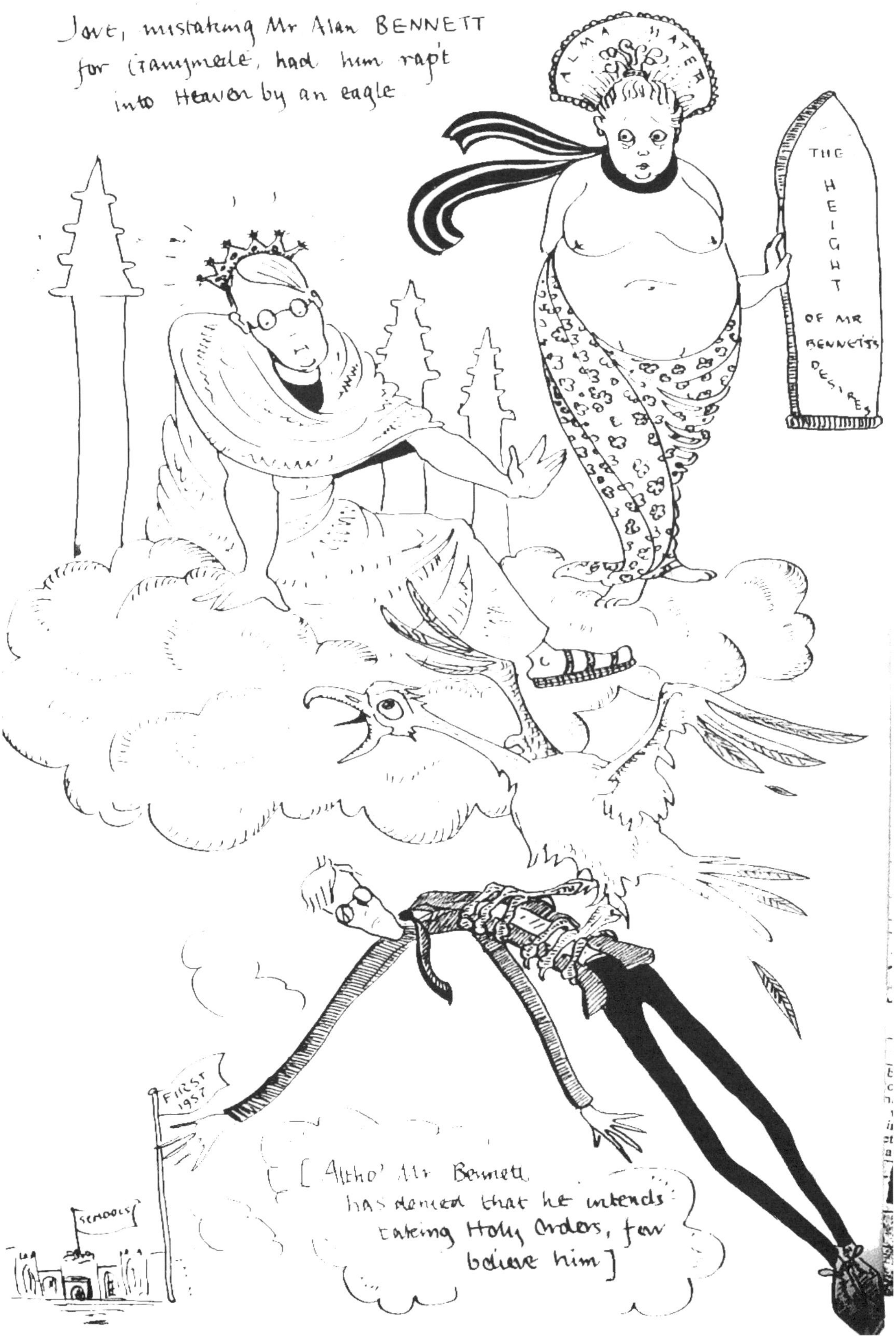
Jove, mistaking Mr Alan BENNETT for Ganymede, had him rapt into Heaven by an eagle
ALMA MATER
THE HEIGHT OF MR BENNETT'S DESIRES
FIRST 1957
SCHOOLS
[Altho' Mr Bennett has denied that he intends taking Holy Orders, few believe him]

Yrs, John Morley
(Hilary '58)

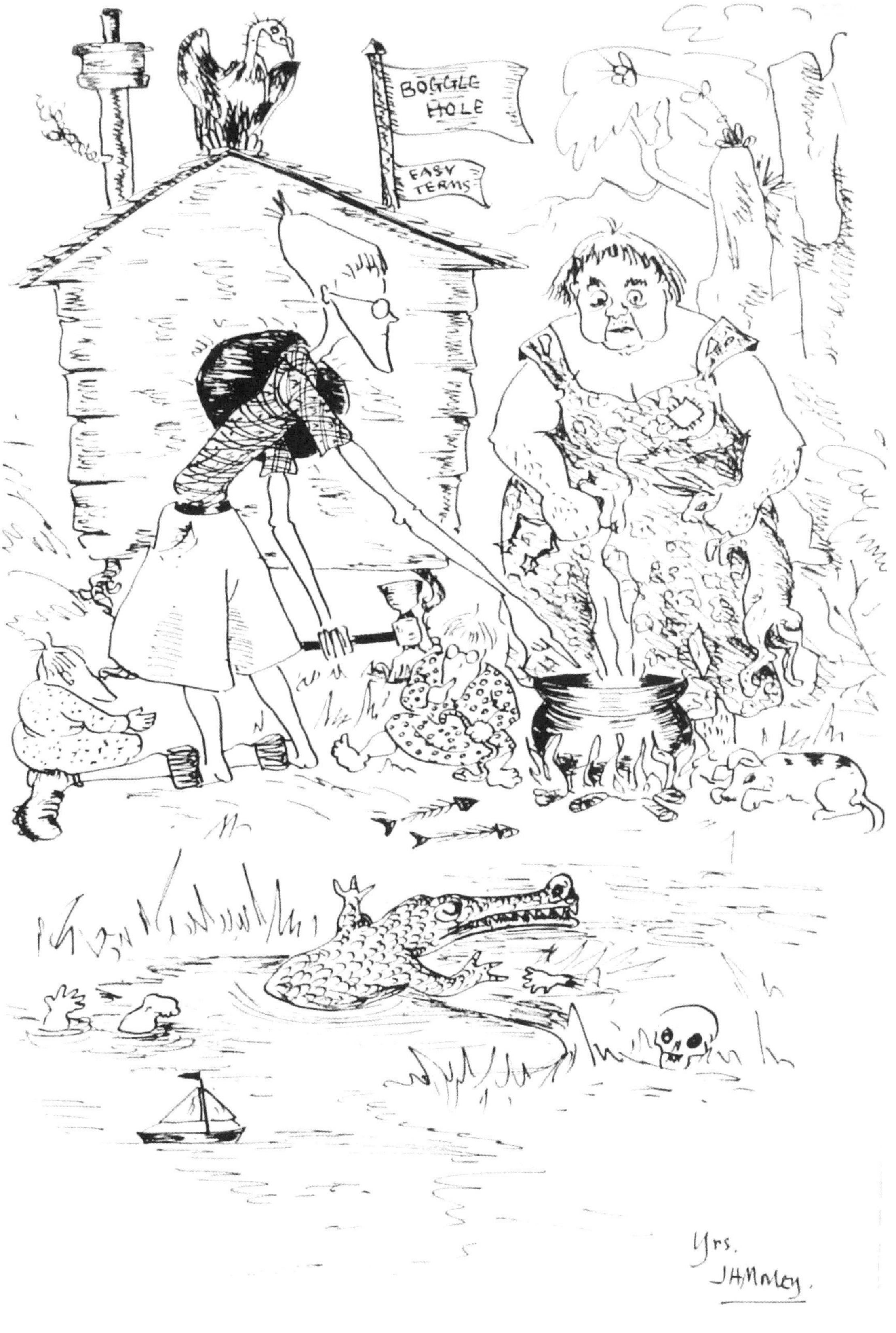
BOGGLE HOLE
EASY TERMS
Yrs.
JHMorley.

(Hilary '58)

Sir,

> Bennett, Bennett, burning bright,
> Wedder's book in hand at night,
> Taking Micky left and right,
> Is it witty – or just spite?
>
> With what skill you take the p**s,
> Those shafts and snakes which never miss.
> The cliques, the chaps – you see them all,
> But isn't this – well, rather small?
>
> As Man to Man we must insist,
> Did thou who got a First write this?
>
>> Yours enquiringly,
>> ANON
>> p.p. ABC XYZ

President's reply:

> Werry Wersatile is he
> Our dearest A (not T) the B
> But Sir it really isn't on
> To sign yourself just plain Anon.
>> AAI Wedderburn
>> (Trinity '58)

Sir,

In response to the freshman's – "Oh! but I thought the President of the J.C.R. was always good at sport" – perhaps you can be persuaded to give an exhibition of your hidden talents sometime in the near future.

Yr.

RW Johnson.

P.S. Anyway what gave him the idea you weren't "good at sport?"

(Michaelmas '58)

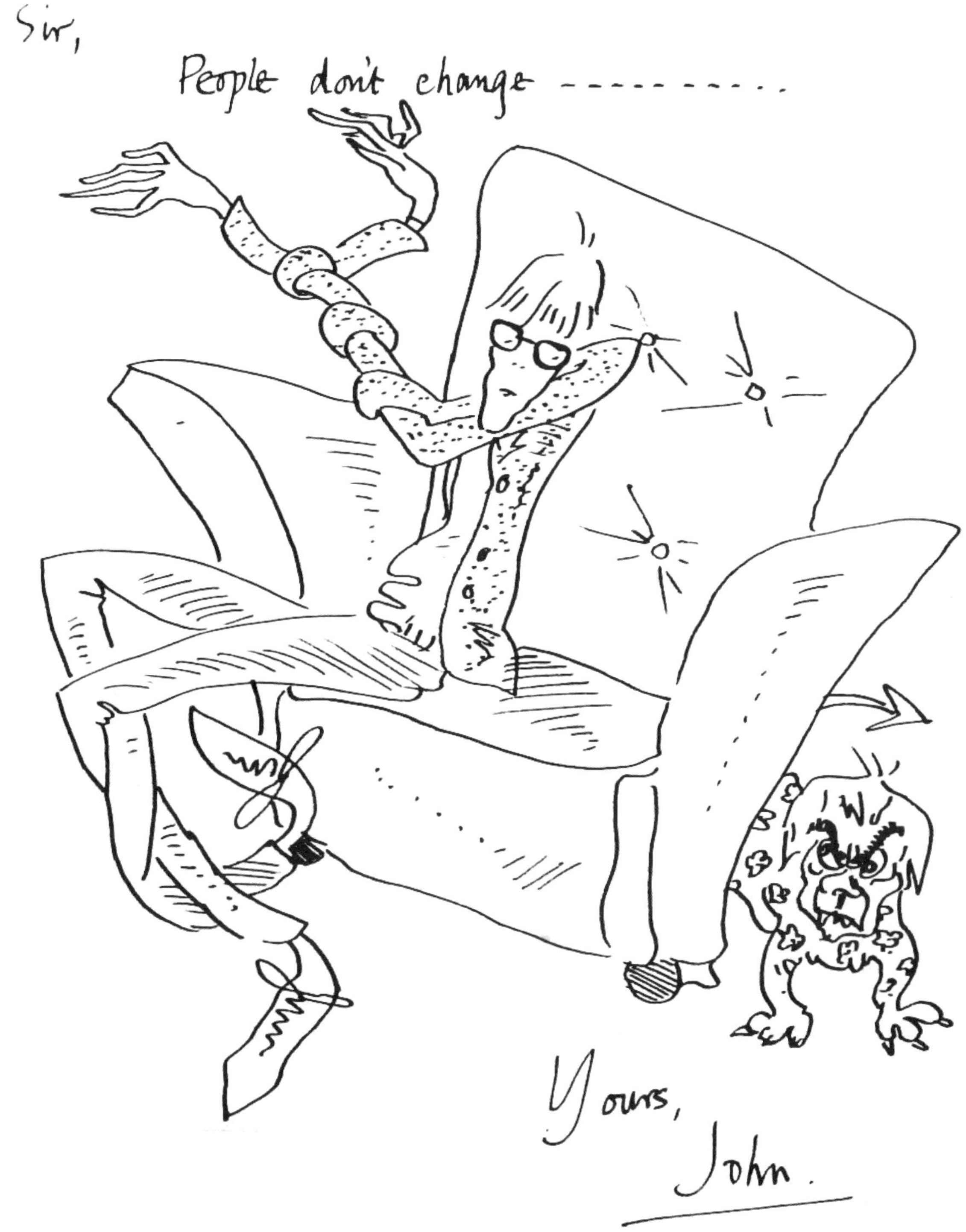
Sir,
People don't change ....
Yours,
John.

John Morley
(Trinity '59)

Dear Sir,

C.S. Lewis and I will be bringing out in the near future an edition of "The Epistles of Paul to the Exonians". They are a remarkable collection. The original thinking which marks the earlier epistles (already published) is wholly absent; in fact, these are quite remarkable for their naivete. Spelling and punctuation will, of course, be modernised.

Yrs,
DG Vaisey

Sir,

It has been my good fortune to take into my hands an advance copy of the above work. You will no doubt remember the paeans of justified panegyric which greeted his first work and I am glad to be able to say that the same sure scholarly eye has perused and arranged these truly incomparable letters. The Senior Tutor handed me the book and I aver, Sir, that he wiped a tear – of joy surely – from his kindly cheek as he said, "Take it: Cicero has met his match after all these centuries. Truly I shall die happy."

This work is indeed unparalleled: when shall we see such zeitgeist again? Dr Vaisey has cut his way through what was often a bewildering fabric of contradictions: in addition to explanation of obscure references he has had the ingenious notion of linking the letters with relevant passages from the Daily Worker. What emerges is a more than usually interesting psychological study: it is the picture of a man, of a generation, of Life itself. Sir, I urge you, when next you go to Paris, obtain a copy and smuggle it back. It will be more than worth the fine.

Yours,
David Authers

Dear Sir,

The other day I was having a friendly chat in the JCR with someone – don't know his name, nice chap though – and the conversation turned, as conversation will, on Justice, Peace, Truth and Righteousness. And blow me! It emerged we both believed in Brotherhood Among Nations! I was rather staggered by this, I must say. I mean, perhaps I seem naïve, but you know, I assumed this was something I'd thought of by myself, forged it out of my own experience, as it were. But no. Here was someone sitting beside me in the JCR who'd come on the same idea independently. Do you know, I was thrilled. And I had a thought. Perhaps all over the world, chaps, white ones, black ones, perhaps even ones who don't speak English, may have been working out this idea in their own lives themselves. And that all we need to do is speak out and then all the people who've been thinking like this will recognise each other. And what's the result? World Peace. It's as simple as that.

So that's why I've written this letter. Just to make myself known. And I'd like to ask everyone else who believes in World Brotherhood to write in this book, then we'll know where we stand. Perhaps then we can do something positive about it. Read each other's magazines or get ourselves a badge or something.

Yrs etc,
Alan Bennett
(Hilary '60)

〰

Sir,

It's very interesting to find – writing I may say, because I've nothing better to do, aimlessly, without attempting a 'compact and worthwhile creation' [send this in as a slogan for Maidenform bras] – it's very interesting, as I was saying, to find that you regard the letters in this book as the raw material of art – which, transmuted onto the walls of the cellar, or the pages of the Stapeldon magazine, would ipso facto become Art. I've been urging this idea on Morley for a long time now, telling him he ought to find better vehicles for his talent than this book and, putting it delicately, the slobs who read it. I only hope your injunctions have more effect than mine.

Yours etc,
Alan Bennett

Sir,

Mr. Bennett's new stream-of-consciousness style is very interesting. He could produce something New in theses. Yrs etc JHMorley.

Sir,

Those, surely.

Yrs etc. ABennett.

It's a long time since I drew him.

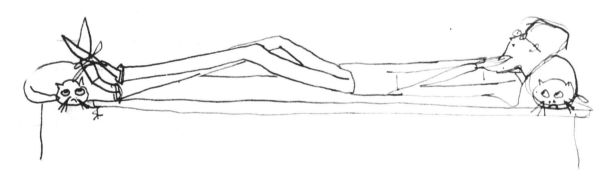

Sir,

Mr. Bennett's drawing looks remarkably like a design for his tombstone. Is Mr.Bennett a morbid man?

Yrs etc,
D. Williams

Sir,

He looks like an Olde Type Crusader home from the wars.

Yrs etc

JH Morley

P.S. I'm sorry I wrote this, because on closer examination that's obviously what he meant it to be. But I feel that the baroque-type is more in his line__

(with apologies to Country Life)

Yrs etc,

JH Morley

(Trinity '58)

Chapter 6
Derek Whitelock

Derek Whitelock came up to Exeter in 1954 at the same time as Alan Bennett. They had met while doing National Service, but had not warmed to each other. They were therefore not pleased to discover that they would be sharing a room in College (double rooms had a living room with two small bedrooms attached).

Derek was a regular contributor to the JCR Books – mainly through letters, but his unique style was also expressed through some entertaining cartoons. The story line was shared fairly equally between words and drawings. The words were legible on the foolscap page of the JCR Books, but only intermittently so when reduced to fit A4 paper. As a result, it has been necessary to divide Derek's cartoons into their component parts, thus enabling them to be enhanced in size. Where possible the names of the main characters are shown below the cartoons. Most of them had Adrian [Nick] Bedson and Brian Brindley as the main characters. Alan Bennett also appears regularly, and in his final cartoon Derek forecasts Alan's future fame.

The first short cartoon expounds the fame of a colleague FJ Roper, who appears again in the first letter of Chapter 10.

(Hilary '55)

[Sir - As Bullfighter; "Olé... Olé"]
[- Swashbuckler; "Aaaarggh"]
[and Lover...; "Caramba!"]
[Who can compare with El Ropero, the Curse of Castile; Yrs DA Whitelock]

Sir,

Now that we're all feeling vernal, what about a Pleasure Dome in the quad? Designed, of course, by Mr. Brindley, built of blue-veined marble, full of Nubian flunkeys and lithe Creole women, and piles of peach blossom: with pools alive with red fish; and peacocks, and humming birds; and birds of paradise flying through the lotus trees. Saha!

Yrs,

DA Whitelock

Brian Brindley
(Hilary '55)

Sir / I append the Battle of Caribou Rib, a Saga of the Mid West

[Into the peaceful little Burg of Caribou Rib, Sask. (Saskatchewan, province of Canada), rides 'Mex' Brindley, the last of the badmen.]

[The honest cow pokes scatter; "Mex Brindley's in town!"]
[Even 'Prettyboy' Ogilvy, the mountie, flees]

[Brindley swaggers into the saloon]
["Gimme a redeye"]

[Then the Ruffian notices Sairie Lou, the prairie flower]
[And begins to pester her; "C'mon you sweet l'il chaw of tobaccy, let's live"]

[Then a quiet, level voice cuts through the air]
["Ah wouldn't do that if ah wuz you, Brindley"]

[It is 'Gent' Mitchell, from the Bar ... Y]

[They fight frenziedly]
["Aargh"; "Bop"; "Splat"; "Ugh"]

(Hilary '55)

[Until Mex is soundly thrashed, handed over to 'Blackfeet' Guram, the Sheriff, and lynched. 'Gent' rides into the sunset wirh Sairie Lou, watched by the admiring Caribou Ribbers.]
["Ah'm a leavin' Cheyenne"; "Thet guy deserves tuh go tuh Awxford"]

[As you all know, dynamic, rock-jawed Nick is investigating the Case of the Madagascan spronje. He is just rescuing Sepia de la Rue, wealthy nymphomaniac in a saw-mill in Prague when...]
["But Nick! Can't you think of any way for me to thank you?"; "Stash the soft stuff doll! Let's blow."]

[The door opens, and in comes Lopez Brindley, dillettante dope-pedlar, and his hoods - Graves, French, Bennett and Maisel, all names written in blood and flame in the annals of crime.]
["We got company babe"; "This calls for violence I fear my dears"; "Grab sky mister"]

[Nick fights like a cougar but...]
["Splat"; "Pow"]

(Michaelmas '55)

[He is black-jacked from behind by snow addict Graves and flung into a cage with Brindley's pet boa-constrictor, Walter.]
[Meanwhile, over in Exeter College, Mike Sissons is drunk again...]

THE DIVERTING EXPERIENCES OF DEVEREUX FITz BED, GENTLEMAN

The place — White's Club, social nucleus of Regency London. Devereux FitzBed, celebrated fop, rake, and roué is playing faro with Sir Joscelyn Ffowl-Ffeend Brindley, bart., whose gothick mansion, Pusey Towers, is the scene of many a rightful orgy. Watching tensely are Cornet Pretheringhulme-Partridge (of the Fifth) the Duke of Short, 'Buck' Christin, Bishop Graves, Lord Close, 'Beau' Clements, Mr. French, and Maisel. Sir Joscelyn is losing, and drinking, heavily. The atmosphere is taut.

[The place - White's Club, social nucleus of Regency London. Devereux Fitzbed, celebrated fop, rake, and roué is playing faro with Sir Joscelyn Ffowl-Ffeend Brindley, bart., whose gothick mansion, Pusey Towers, is the scene of many a rightful orgy. Watching tensely are Cornet Pretheringhulme-Partridge (of the Fifth) the Duke of Short, 'Buck' Christin, Bishop Graves, Lord Close, 'Beau' Clements, Mr. French, and Maisel. Sir Joscelyn is losing, and drinking, heavily. The atmosphere is taut.]

Graves	Close	Clements	Christin	Brindley	Partridge
French	Bedson	Short			
Maisel					

["Ho! Ho! Not doin' well Brinders! What?"]

[Suddenly Devereux notices that Brindley is cheating. Coldly he flings a pail of wine into his wicked visage.]
["You cur, Sir Joscelyn!"; "Faugh!"]

[A duel is arranged the following dawn.]
["I'll put you chaps in the picture. When I say 'Okay chaps!' you start walking to the count of 10, then bang away. Ho! Ho! Ho! Got it? Okay, chaps!"]

[But hardly has the gallant cornet reached, with some difficulty, the count of 5 than Brindley wheels round and pistols Fitzbed!]
["Heh! Heh!"]

[The spectators are horrified.]
["Serve him right"; "Good Gad! Not on Brindley!"; "Demme!"; "He must be in terrible pain"; "Stap me!"]
[But Devereux despite his desperate wound remains standing and steadily aims his pistol at the insufferable baronet!]

[Meanwhile - on a grassy hill near Liversedge, a flaxen-headed plough-boy is dreaming of the poetry that will one day make him great. It is Bysshe Bennett.]

DA Whitelock
(Hilary '56)

Sir,

DECLINE AND FALL OF OLD EXONIANS.
A SERIES OF TRUE LIFE ADVENTURES

Case I Monsignor Brindley

1974 Brindley at last leaves Exeter College. After a vivid BBC career (Housewives' Choice, Children's Hour, Chats with Brindley) joins (1976) an obscure, exclusive order of Epicurean crypto-Jesuists. Astonishing rise in Vatican, widely acclaimed for his interest in youth, Cook prize for Most Eminent Benefactor to Humanity. Then ruin – unpleasant revelations by Duncan Webb disguised as Cardinal. Mgr Brindley accused by "People" and Mr. Blewitt of Sodomy, casuistry, masochism and Zoroastism. Flees to Seychelles. Combs beaches.

Yrs,
DA Whitelock

Mgr Brindley at his prime   Mgr Brindley in decline

Sir, Decline and Fall, case (ii)

BYSSHE BENNETT

Brilliant first, refuses fellowship to C*RIS* CH*RCH. Ousts B*V*RLY NI*HO*S in 'Womens' Own'! Sensational success of publications 'Sense and Sensitivity', 'U', "Gold and Velvet", "My friend Graves", "Confessions of an Aesthete", 'Oh My Lord!' and 'Poesy' and 'Thoughts' (a collection of poems bound in mauve vellum). Awarded Mr. R*OSEVE*T Prize for Literature. Hailed by Godfrey W*NN as 'The lonely W*OLF'. Approached by M.*.M. Turns back on fame at 29 and becomes shepherd in Upper Swaledale. Tells reporters 'I have found Truth'.

Yrs,

DA Whitelock

(Trinity '56)

THE VALOROUS EXPLOITS OF SIR BARNABAS BEDDESSONE, KNIGHT

Sire!

The year is 1213. King John Plantabrindley, egged on by his effeminate favourites, Piers Partridge and Benet the Jester, has just finished reading a proclamation making himself Pope & Holy Roman Emperor to his cowed magnates

Bennett   Brindley   Partridge

[Sire! The year is 1213. King John Plantabrindley, egged on by his effeminate favourites, Piers Partridge and Benet the Jester, has just finished reading a proclamation making himself Pope & Holy Roman Emperor to his cowed magnates.]
["Ho! Ho! Ho!"]

[Then up spake bold Sir Barnabas...]
["Bie Goddes Teeth Sir Kyng ere I bow mine proude hied to sic Tyrrannie I will to Scottelond flee"; "Bie Goddes Bloode Fals Knight you wil perish for this iniquitie!"]

[The barons of the court ride after Sir Barnabas.]
[All except the Seigneurde Sissoons, the Bastard of Easingwold, who is drunk.]
["Ye wold nat nob it!"]

[Riding like the wind, Sir Barnabas shakes off his pursuers and reaches the Cheviots. Suddenly a huge, hairy Pict appears. It is Muckle Wedder o' the Burn.]
["Bie the bonie hairs o' St. Andrew's hied, by the laverock ayint the lea, bie the carking bannocks o moonlicht nichts, O, I will fecht with thee"; "Ye Goddes"]

(Michaelmas '59)

[Meanwhile, in a monastery near Heckmondwike, an ambitious and lugubrious young monk is putting deadly night shade berries in the saintly old abbot's soup. It is Brother Graves.]

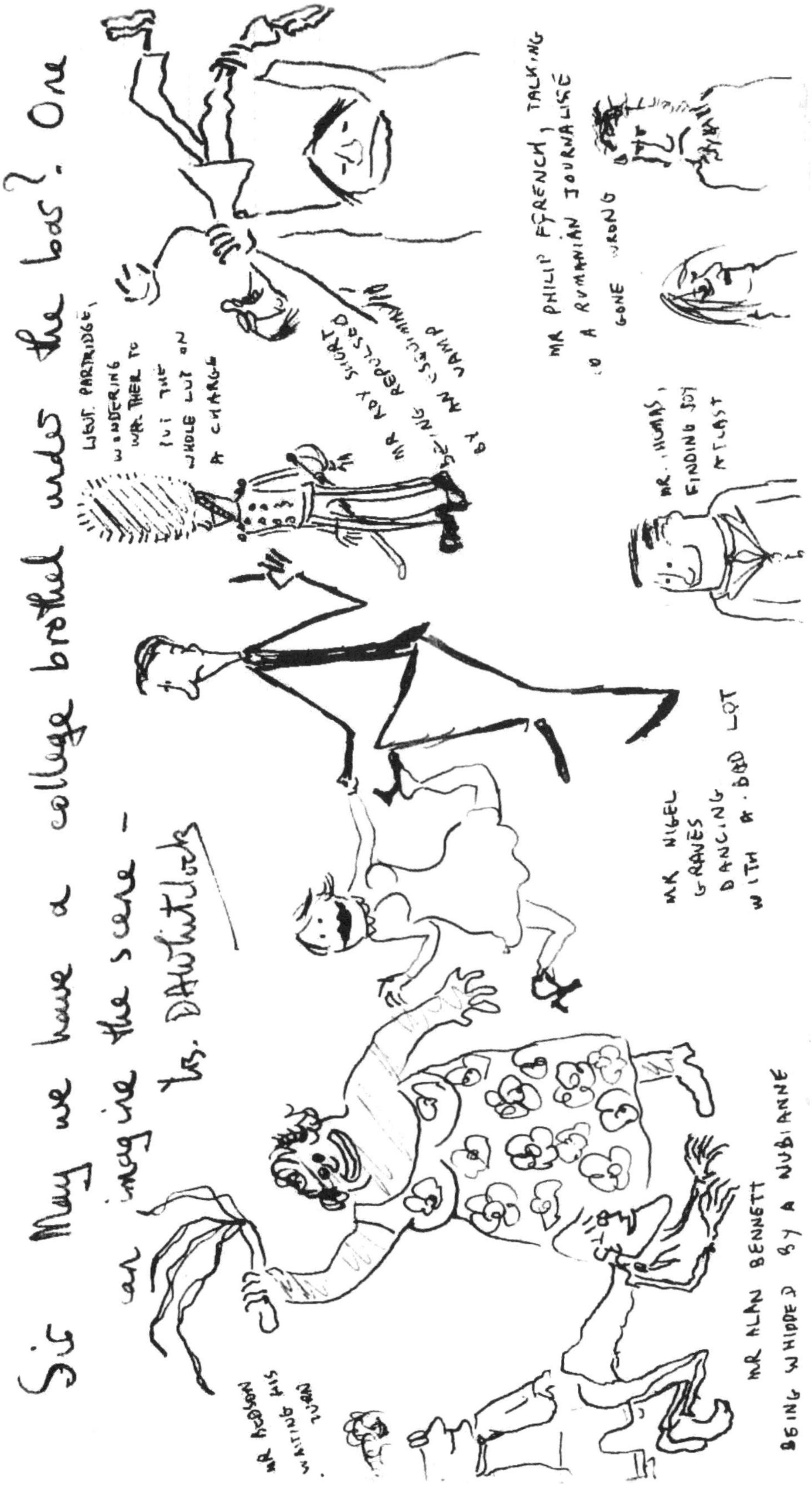
Sir May we have a college brothel under the bar? One can imagine the scene –
Yrs, DAWhitelock
LIEUT. PARTRIDGE, WONDERING WHETHER TO PUT THE WHOLE LOT ON A CHARGE
MR ROY STUART
MR PHILIP FRENCH, TALKING TO A RUMANIAN JOURNALIST GONE WRONG
MR. THOMAS, FINDING JOY AT LAST
MR NIGEL GRAVES DANCING WITH A BAD LOT
MR ALAN BENNETT BEING WHIPPED BY A NUBIANNE
MR HOBSON WAITING HIS TURN

(Hilary '55)

Chapter 7
College Amenities

The notable College amenities were the dining hall, the chapel, the bar, the library, the Morris Room, the College garden and the bathroom facilities. Some of them were taken for granted and not often mentioned in the JCR Books. However there are numerous letters about the Morris Room and the library, and even more about the bathroom facilities.

It is, in retrospect, an extraordinary fact that in 1955 there were no baths or WCs available for the use of undergraduates other than underground at the far end of the College beyond the Back Quad. This location was referred to as the fourth or Forth or Fforth Quad. There was no agreement on how to spell the name, although "fourth" was an unlikely spelling, as the College only had two quadrangles – the Front Quad and the Back Quad.

The Fforth Quad (the most popular spelling) was a continual source of trouble and complaint. Either it was flooded (leading to calls on the Captain of Punts to provide equipment to reach the facilities), or there was no hot water available for baths. There was a College servant, whose job was to keep the Fforth Quad clean and operating satisfactorily. During the period covered by this book, the first man was called Jack the Bathman (or J. the B.) and the second Wally. Both are referred to in a number of amusing letters – J. the B. as if he were the bathman referred to in Aristophanes' play 'The Frogs'; and Wally as writing a thesis on 'The American Approach to the Philosophy of Hygiene and Sanitation' following a holiday in the USA. Each year the Stapeldon Society elected a member as Lord High Commissioner of Public Easement (LHCPE). Some eminent men were holders of this troublesome post, for example two Presidents, Ned Sherrin and Brian Brindley.

In 1956/57 the College installed a WC at the foot of a staircase in the Front Quad. This was named the Star Chamber after the ceiling paper. The need for colleges to raise money by hosting conferences etc in the vacations had exposed Exeter's medieval facilities. The installation of baths and WCs thereafter on every staircase led to the removal of chamber-pots from the bedrooms. There is no reference to this in any of the JCR letters, though the installation of an automatic hand-dryer in the Star Chamber led to numerous ribald letters. There are also a few letters aimed at providing acceptable facilities for any girl-friends or female relatives visiting the College – they were as antiquated as those in the Fforth Quad.

William Morris and Edmund Burne-Jones, two of the most eminent members of the Pre-Raphaelite Movement, met in Exeter College as undergraduates. At some point the room between the JCR and the SCR was named the Morris Room and decorated appropriately with his wall-paper, curtains, tapestries and tiles, and two drawings of Flora and Pomona by Burne-Jones. The room was used for studying and social meetings by undergraduates. From the many letters about the Morris Room have been chosen a sample deploring all aspects of its decoration, its use as a store by out-of-college undergraduates for their clothes and bags, and its general shoddy state.

The College library, a separate Victorian building behind the JCR and overlooking the lovely College garden, was the main place used for studying, apart from undergraduates' rooms and

University libraries such as the Bodleian. Virtually every year, come the winter, there were letters complaining about the lack of adequate heating. In the summer the letters tended to be complaints about noise – probably reflecting panic as "Schools" (i.e. final exams) loomed.

Sir,

Is the LHCPE doing anything about the slowly disintegrating cistern in the slash-house?
Yours,
P.A. Spring

Sir,

As Lord High Commissioner for Public Easement it is my unpleasant duty to exercise my mind on a letter by Mr P.A. Spring. I am not sure if Mr Spring has served his time with the Colours already or whether this pleasure is in store for him. However, if he is to use military slang in this book would he please make sure that it is correct slang? Here he should either say Slash-Pit or (and I write this with modest misgivings) SHIT-house.

I suspect that Mr. Spring's visits to my sphere of influence are few and far between; let me assure him that my interest in my job is all consuming. Every gurgle is a matter of my personal concern, every drain that laughs gives me butterflies in the stomach.

This particular cistern is under the fatherly care of the Clerk of the Works or whatever the fellow's name is who is paid to act as a sort of Nanny to all the Lavatories (I trust that any more mature member of the JCR will excuse the simple homely phrases I am using to bring my point home to Mr Spring).

If Mr Spring would like any more information about our own beloved Public Easement Block or about Lavatories in general I shall be pleased to tell all (free of charge). May I suggest that Mr Spring takes advantage of the new Travelling Lavatory Research Scholarship so generously instituted by the JCR at its last meeting.
Yours,
E.G. Sherrin

Sir,

Hope Spring's eternal.
Yours,
D.B. Williams

Sir,

To Pun
Is fun,
But Spring's
A Thing
That has been slightly overdone
Yours,
E.G. Sherrin

Sir,

I suggest respectfully
That the L.H.C.P.E.
Confine his wit
To shit.
Yours,
D.B. Williams

Sir,

You are spent, Daffydd Williams
I grieve to say
And your verse is fast losing its bite
Go back to your kennel and quietly pray
"Please Heaven teach Dai how to write."
Yours,
E.G. Sherrin

Sir,

Your rhyming appals, Sir.
Your phrasing is worse
The lavat'ry wall, Sir
'S the place for your verse.
Yours,
D.B. Williams

Sir,

What a horrible thought
To suggest that I ought
To try to keep time
In halting rhyme,
With all the things
That Williams slings
In this book__
__But look;
As a parting shot
To clinch the lot,
In the language of verse,
Reversed and terse,
I will say this
--OFF PISS.
Yours,
E.G. Sherrin

In the whole of this college
O, where could we find
Another man of our knowledge
With such a low mind?
Yours
D.B. Williams
(Hilary '52)

Sir,

I am delighted by the interest exhibited by the members of the J.C.R. in the question of bathing facilities. The bath is an institution which – although it may have known better times – has fallen on evil days in this country. At least, so it would appear to those of us approaching England from a more sanitary side of the Atlantic.

Yours sincerely,

D.A. Mitchell

Sir,

I resent the suggestion of the contributor with the uneducated handwriting that we are an insanitary community. I personally take a bath regularly once a term, whether I need it or not, and I believe some members of the college bathe even more frequently than this.

Yrs,

R.C. Barton

Sir,

I have just waded into the College urinals. Could you please ask the LHCPE to get his punt out and paddle down to see if he can unblock the drains. It would be a pity if some luckless inebriate were to drown there.

Yrs,

HFM Thomas
(Michaelmas '52)

Sir,

A dialogue entitled STAR CHAMBER

Exonian
"All Blessings on the Bursar who
Has built a loo
On staircase 2.
Another nears its finished state
I'm pleased to state
On staircase 8
And, I'm told, there are some more
There's half a score
On staircase 4."

Rector
Fforth-with remove the ancient loo!
The space will do
For you know who
With timber from the College barge
To build a large
Private garage."

Your humble servant,
Michael Imison
(Michaelmas '57)

Sir,

I have always taken rather a dim view of "Jack the Bathman," but now it has all come to light. Busily working away in the library I found a reference to J. the B. in Aristophanes' "Frogs," and therefore estimate his age at about 2,382. May I quote the reference? Lines 708 sqq., translated as follows:

"Not long shall that little buffoon,
That Cleigenes shifty and small, the wickedest bathman of all
Who are lords of the earth – which is brought from the isle
Of Cimolius and wrought
With nitre and lye into soap –
Not long shall he vex us, I hope." (Rogers)

Rogers adds the note; "He is here described as a worthless and quarrelsome little bathman, but.. we may be sure that he was a politician of the same type as Cleophon, and therefore an opponent of peace.. The bath business was probably his father's trade."

On this evidence I fear the attempts to get the paintwork and duck-boards seen to will come to nought. Apart from being a dishonest dealer he is also, it seems, an anarchic revolutionary, nay more, a spy. Beware the Ides of March.

Yrs. fearfully,
MA Sharpe

Sir,

Ref........"busily working away in the library I found a reference".........
What was a reference doing busily working away in the library?
Yrs etc,
DE Garrood

Sir,

Perhaps it was a cross reference working off its anger.
M Brown

Sir,

References when mixed up are best taken to the sea-side for a rest cure.
You see, littoral translations are sometimes advantageous.
Anonymous
[BW Coulson]

Sir,

This has gone quite far enough. The groans are even now resounding through the JCR.
NR Graves
(Hilary '57)

Sir,

A proposed addition to the College. A covered walk from it to the bar would be a further improvement.

Yrs etc,
JH Morley

Sir,

What an absolutely splendid idea of Mr. Morley's! (It is I hope, meant to be a shit-house – if not, it can easily be converted). This splendid, titful bit of rococo would gladden the bleary old eyes on many a grey and shaky morning. I demand that it be erected as a monument, if not to posterity, at least to the artistic spirit of our sleazy old college.

Yrs,
Dad O'Callaghan
(Trinity '57)

Sir,

The Star-Chamber, after being cleaned out thoroughly this morning, smells now like the parrot-house at the zoological gardens. Is this an aphrodisiac?

Yours sincerely

M Seakins

No, Sir, it is "Soirée de Hong Kong " par Jacques-Jasper Chevalier.

For the sophisticated, however, we recommend the same house's "Essence Aromatique des Bean Shoots."

Malc. (Malcolm Brown)

(Hilary '58)

Sir,

As a former Lord High Commissioner for Publick Easement, Rear-Admiral, Privy-Councillor, Master of the Rolls, Clerk of the Closet (Royal Victorian Chain), Burgomaster of Flushing, Honorary Freeman of the Boroughs of Love Pennycomequick and Piddle-in the-Hole, all of which posts I venture to say I adorned, until compelled to resign my seat, it grieves me to see the House of Israel whoring after strange gods. The Star Chamber, Sir, is all very well, but what about the Fforth Benefaction? I was shocked: paint peeling, copper pipes unpolished, fitments fastened with string, the hand-towel a sodden mess! Mrs Fforth must be turning in her urn!. Is this piety? Is it gratitude? Is it even decency? This is no academic point – the Fforth Quad is exposed to other eyes than yours; what of the Young Ladies looking for the Lower Lecture Room? What of the Young Ladies looking for Staircase IX? What of the Young Ladies looking for you or for the Rector? What of the Young Ladies looking for the Joan Wheare Room? Research has shown that the Fforth Quad is the Male Preserve most frequented by Accidental Women per man-hour for its area in Oxford. The Good Name of the College is At Stake.

Yrs etc,

Brian Brindley

(Hilary '58)

Sir !

A serious complaint. The ladies' lavatory in this College is in a disgraceful state. It has been for years. Can you PLEASE see that action is taken, and kept up.

Yrs Malc.

Sir,

      Why is Mr. Brown interested in the Ladies' lavatory? The surgeon's knife has cut deep indeed.

Yrs etc.
J H Morley

(Hilary '57)

Sir,

Mr. Homessy wishes to alter a national monument.

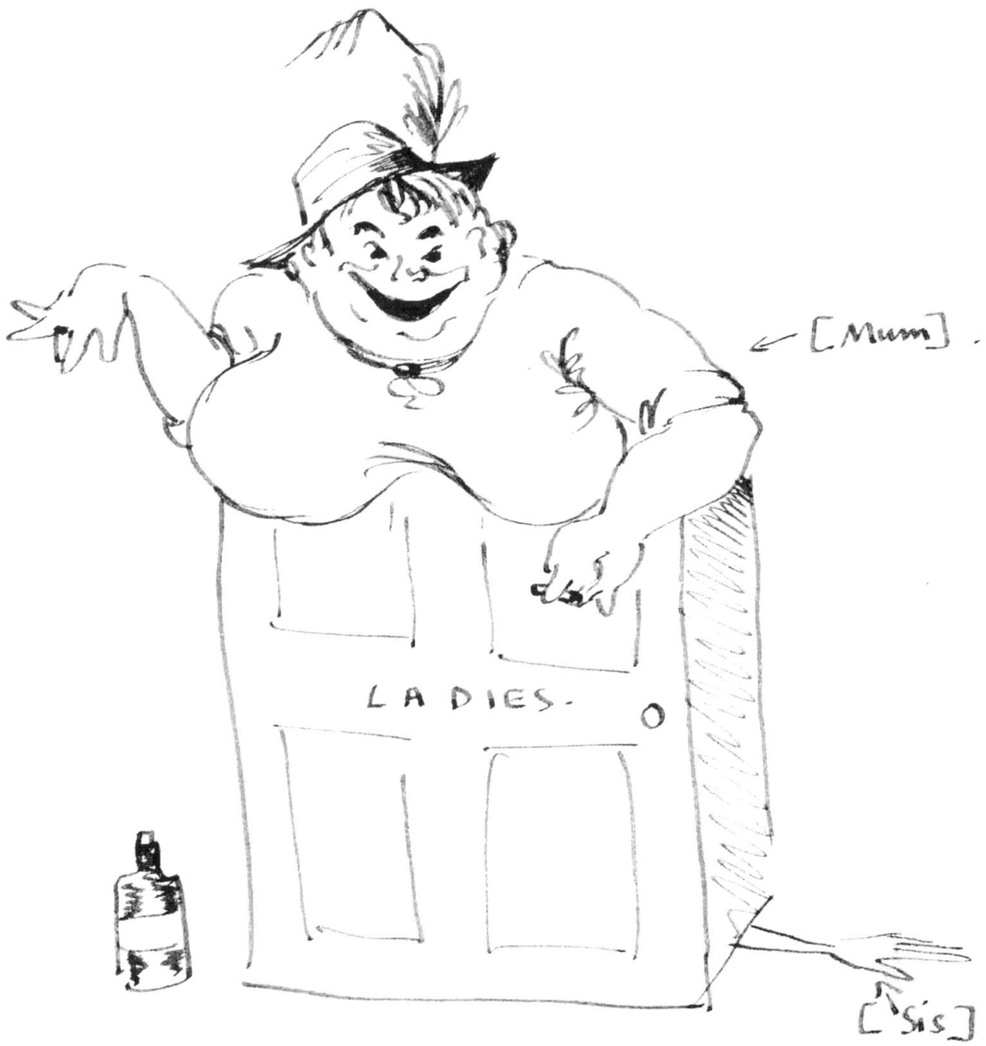
[Mum].
LADIES.
[Sis]

Modernisation is never aesthetic.

Yrs etc. J.H. Morley.

(Hilary '57)

Sir,

I am not boastful. I am not proud. The automatic tool-dryer in the Star Chamber is <u>too high</u> for me.

Please lower it (a) One foot, between Tuesday and Friday
(b) 18ins, after week-ends
Yours convalescently
Malc Brown,

Sir,

If you don't wash your hands first, the oojah in the bog is very efficient as a hand-warmer. We might have a towel as well, then we could warm our clean hands.
Malcolm Brown

Sir,

Mr. Beechey should try to imagine an oojah without a hole in it.
BW Coulson

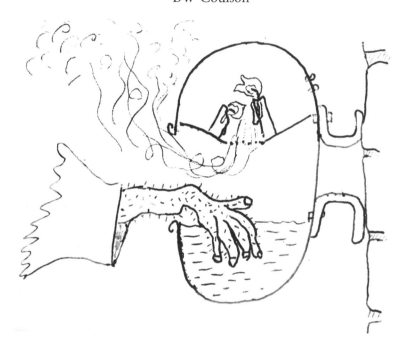

Sir,

One aspect of the drying of hands by the use of the hand-drier which seems to have been overlooked is that the evaporation of 1 gram of water (equivalent to 1/1480 lb or 1/600 pint) at normal winter temperatures requires the absorption of the vast amount of about 640 calories of heat energy. Considerations involving the average values of say, 2ccs of water per pair of maulers, an efficiency of, say, 40% by the machine, deterioration of the machine and inconvenience because it doesn't remove soap, dehydrates the skin etc, and comparison of all this with mere dhobeying of towels at perhaps 4 1/2p, I will leave to the reader. I like a nice crisp towel, even if it is crisp only once a week.

Yours sincerely,
Michael Seakins
(Michaelmas '57)

Sir,

The season of mists and mellow fruitfulness is so to speak upon us again: the smog swirls, the traffic stalls and no birds sing. But, Sir, Mother Nature is a generous lady: for though the proverbial brazen apes are fearful for their virility there is also beauty. Have you noticed the wonder of the Camera viewed through a tracery of the branches and twigs of trees in the College Garden? In the Meadows and Parks the trees remind us of the ageless thisness of things: they provide shelter for our little feathered friends and provide a nice setting for chaps to take pictures of the odd tot. But, Sir, we must not become too sentimental: trees, eternal though they seem, are after all only a crop and like all crops they have their seedtime and harvest: they are planted, spring up, achieve maturity and are harvested by men. So, Sir how about it: I know that we live in a Scientific Age, when the Flag of Knowledge is ever being staked in hitherto undiscovered Realms of Opinion: I know too that what the scientist can do with plastics is wondrous indeed. But, Sir, he cannot make a comfortable bog-seat. The icy clutch of one of those plastic wotsits on a cold winter's morn takes all joy from the performance of one of what should be the most pleasurable of man's functions: it is in winter especially that we feel the need for the comfort of a good timber seat. Yet both in the ffilthy fforth and in the subterranean Places of Easement there is far too small a proportion of wooden seats. I appeal to you, Sir, to look to our comfort: badger the bursar and tell the clerk of the works that when it comes to bog-seats there just is no substitute for wood.

Yours,
David Authers

Sir,

Wally is in Oxford. He was seen a few days back entering the New Bod where he is engaged in writing a thesis. The title is "The American Approach to the Philosophy of Hygiene and Sanitation."

Yours,
Oswyn Murray

Sir,

With reference to Mr Murray's letter, I can confirm that Wally is back and studying amongst us once again. I saw him coming out of the library with a copy of Aristotle's "Posterior Analytics" and he told me how much he was enjoying getting right back to the sources to find out if the Greeks did have a word for it. In order to familiarise himself thoroughly with the Grandeur that was Greece he is daily to be seen dressed in a chiton and pouring a libation to the great god Pan before dawn in the Fourth: he says his favourite character in Greek literature is Arsinoe. He says that while in America he had been studying under (if you see what I mean) Al Capone's brother Al Kaseltzer but considered him nothing but a windbag – especially after reading his paper "De Gustibus." Dr Wally has written a semi-autobiographical article, to be published in the forthcoming "Festschrift" in honour of the 70th birthday of Dr Augustus Q. Krapperberger," (U.Y.B. 37/6), in which he justifies the use of timber in the construction of closet covers: he confesses that apart from an unfortunate encounter with a splinter while at Uppingham he has nothing but warm feelings and fragrant memories in connection with wooden bog-seats.

D.J. Authers
(Trinity '58)

Sir,

What is that revolting piece of ersatz carpet adorning the Morris Room? One presumes it is an example of Morris's work, could you tell me when it was bought, why it was bought, and whether there is any hope of getting rid of it?

JM Ashworth

P. S. It would make a jolly good bathroom mat.

President's reply:

Your obvious ignorance hardly excuses the boorishness of this letter. The tapestries were the property of Nevill Coghill, and he has given them to the college to hang in the Morris Room. When a fellow of the college has devoted so much energy and money to providing a fitting memorial of one of the greatest products of this college, it is ungracious, to say the least, to greet the latest evidence of his generosity in the manner you adopt.

NR Graves

Sir,

My attention has been drawn to your reply to Mr. Ashworth's remarks on the Morris Room tapestries.

Mr. Ashworth, if I understand him correctly, said the tapestries were ugly, like bathroom mats. You said; (1) William Morris is one of the greatest products of this college. (2) Mr Coghill has spent a great deal of time and money on the Morris Room.

Even Mr Boulter can see that there is a logical error here. Mr Ashworth is talking, and rightly talking, in terms of bathmats, you in terms of reputations, hard work, merit.

But leaving this lapsus mentis on one side I can only heartily concur with Mr. A. As the guardian of the artistic heritage of this college I think the Morris Room is hideous. I know Gothic is smart (vide Messer Brindley, Clements, Morley and Anderson) but O! those curtains! And the wallpaper! (vide monograph on William Morris and Knightsbridge. Better Books 2 shillings and six pence).

Mr. Holden says the Burne Jones drawings are nice. They are rude. That's why he thinks they are nice and the same with Messer. Morley, Clements and Anderson. If they can't get sex anywhere else but the Morris Room it's a pity – Flora and Pomona indeed!

The Archbishop of Canterbury is this college's greatest product (he has 6 sons- 5 are in the regular army, one is a television producer for Granada).

Yrs sincerely,
Alan Bennett

And Felix "my greetings to you both on equal loves great kings of France and England" Aylmer as the next. Then P*tt-R*vers (do the first year people know about this) and the Rector of Stiffkey – some of them don't look as if they do. They ought to be told. (What NHKA Coghill did for Wm Morris, the Old Bailey did for Pitt- Rivers. Discuss) and Wynford Vaughan Thomas. What about him? William Morris indeed! And I wish Mr Morley would stop drawing in this book. He has not a lovely mind. Moreover his excuses for drawing, not suggesting, in this book are patently false.

President's reply

Your attention may have been drawn to my reply, but it has been insufficiently devoted to it. No one has ever suggested that there was any logical connection between the two statements you quote. Whatever you or Mr Ashworth may think of his work, there can be little doubt that Wm Morris was a great artist, and it is fitting that this college should have some memorial of him. To like Gothic is smart now in the same way as it used to be smart to dislike it; whether you like it or not you must admit that the Morris Room is a suitable memorial of the man. This is largely due to the work of Nevill Coghill; and I still maintain that it is ungracious to greet the latest example of his munificence in the manner Mr Ashworth has chosen. Those who dislike the art of Wm Morris are not compelled to look at the Morris Room; those who do like it should be allowed to enjoy this latest evidence of his genius in peace.

NR Graves
(Trinity '57)

Sir,

The problem of the Morris Room is one which has exercised certain of your predecessors as well as yourself, tho' that was before the lovely curtains were put in – and before, incidentally, we had that splendid Burne-Jones in here, which, may I say, I like very much – and it seems that a new approach to the problem is called for. What you need is:

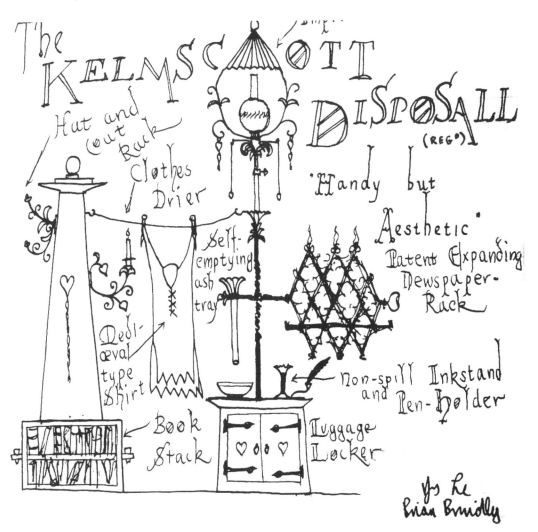

(Hilary '58)

Sir,

If you really want me to quote at full length your own famous tirade against the Morris Room, you had better not attribute your own rhetorical flowers to Mr. Graves of beloved memory. Mr. Graves' reply was of this tone "Morris was a great artist." This was a reply to your own epigram: "Morris was a disgusting mess. It is fitting that his room should be so." You followed up with something about Michael Pitt-Rivers and the Old Bailey, The Rev. FC (Tubby) Clayton, and the Archbishop of Canterbury. I never forget what goes in this book.

Yrs,
Rosie (Ken Rose)

President's reply:

You are of course quite right. I thought no one would remember. It is more than a year ago now. I wrote it – the account of Pitt-River's, Clayton and co – one Wednesday afternoon in June 1957 sat here in front of the fireplace.

But I also remember you won the Brindley prize offered for the reproduction of a letter I once wrote, which had been torn from the book. You ought to leave yourself to the college archives.

Alan Bennett
(Michaelmas '58)

Sir,

I regret your current statement of policy regarding the Morris Room- a centre for third-rate suburban actors, a locale for legal 'moots', whatever they may be, a gymnasium for acrobatics in French colloquial prose. My conception of the Morris Room is somewhere where one can work and smoke concurrently and in fair comfort. You, Sir, must know that creative ability requires congenial environment for its activities. Edith Sitwell can only compose lying down; Victor Hugo needed a soft armchair. I feel my idea of the Morris Room is the nearest approximation to this and a facility which should be available at ALL times.

Yours,
JPH Connell

President's reply:
This is the nicest thing I ever heard said about the Morris Room.

John Moat
(Michaelmas '59)

Sir,

What I really want to write about is the organisation of the College library. Why, Sir, why, a few days before Schools when people are trying to work in the Library, must the Canon come and make the noise that he is making at this minute (3:30 pm). It's bad enough with the pigeons and Mr Bennett anyway, without the Canon dropping books and banging drain pipes together. And this isn't the first time either. Either he's in there turning out, or the catalogue-man and Mrs Nuz. are holding long conversations. It's too bad, Sir, really it is. If it goes on I shan't get my 1st and Mr. Harty won't get his 4th.

Quite seriously, Nigel, will you, or somebody on the Library Committee, point out that it is difficult to work in there when this <u>unnecessary</u> noise is going on. They can very easily turn out or spring clean at some other time, or else tell us when they are going to do so, so that we can keep away.

And another thing I have never understood, is why it is apparently impossible to have the library cleaned before we go in at 9:30 in the morning. The cleaning woman clanging her dust pan doesn't help any. If we had to compete with an army of Mrs. Mops at the Schools this might be good training, but we don't and it isn't.

Good gracious, Sir, I hope my Schools answers come as quickly as this letter has.

Yrs etc,
John P Saunders

Sir,

Schools panic has obviously descended on Mr. Saunders. This is all very amusing for us unsuspecting freshmen but, seriously, our revered Secretary does have a room of his own and there are the Camera and other libraries available to work in. If the Canon's efforts are to result in a cleaner, more up to date and efficient library for those who use it to obtain books to read he should be encouraged not deterred.

Yours,
Michael Imison

Sir,

If Mr. Saunders does not improve his writing pretty soon, his examiners will be writing 'illegible' all over his papers. But, all the same, I agree with him; the Library is also for people to work in, using the books there. And if there was any noise in the Camera or other libraries, complaints would very soon put that right. Mr. Imison's argument is very shaky, and I would point out that long conversations will not help the Canon to make the library cleaner or more efficient; hasn't he got <u>his</u> room for them?

Yours,
JG Speirs

P.S. We are getting depressingly serious.

(Trinity '57)

Sir,

Is there any possibility of warming up the library (college) just a wee bit. People are reduced to using electric lamps for raising the temperature in their immediate proximity.

Yrs,
Gordon Halliday

President's reply:

The College has given formal approval for the renewal and extension of the Library's heating; it should be ready by the summer

The Chaplain informs me that the temperature is supposed to be 65 degrees. If you notice it below, inform the office smartly, and put on your bedsocks.

AAI Wedderburn

President's pictorial reply [Carruthers, the chef's cat, on the ladder and Bennett manning the hose-pipe]

Sir,

Mr Morley is slipping. What I wanted was HEAT not a CARNIVOROUS GROWTH.

Yrs,

Gordon Halliday

(Hilary '58)

Chapter 8
John Morley

John Morley went up to Exeter in 1955 to read Modern History. If the key feature of the golden age of the JCR Books is the drawings, then he was the star. But whereas Brian Brindley was obsessed with everything Gothic and Alan Bennett invariably drew himself, John mainly drew his contemporaries in College and never himself. He was also keen on monsters, which appear in many of his drawings – perhaps he had seen Bosch's paintings at an impressionable age.

One of the joys of John's style of handwriting was that it was beautifully legible, unlike that of so many of the other contributors to the JCR Books. As a result it has been possible to show most of his drawings accompanied by the relevant hand-written letters.

He was always particular about the proper use of the English language, including its spelling. There was a good example in Chapter 2 where Memo Spathis points out, regarding the Broad Gate, that schizophrenia is a psychosis not a neurosis, and John responds that quibble is spelt with two 'b's, not one. He and Alan Bennett sparred with each other, both orally in the JCR and in the Books. There is a fine letter by Alan in Chapter 5 about John Partridge and John Morley engaging in metaphysical squash games. In this case Tim Binyon tells Alan the correct spelling of "deuce" before John Morley has a chance to do it himself!

John was extremely artistic – one of the most successful, if controversial, chairmen of the JCR's Art Committee, as shown in Chapter 2. He had an illustrious career, as an extremely effective Director of Brighton's Museums, as a Curator at the Victoria and Albert Museum, and as an author.

Sir,

Coulson thinks he's a figment of Bedson's imagination. Boulter, however, thinks Coulson is really there. If Morley, however, were a figment of your imagination he would have said so.

We are an extremely intelligent college.

Yrs,

AJ Brooks

'Sir,

If Mr Brookes were a figment of my imagination, I should banish him to the depths of my sub-conscious along with all the other monsters.

Yours etc
F. Coulson

Sir,

On request of Mr. Coulson, the above letter illustrated. I don't vouch for the authenticity of Mr. Brooks, but I do for that of Mr. Coulson's monsters.

Yrs
J H Morley

(Hilary '57)

Sir,

    Apparently there is to be a United Missionary sale in the Town Hall. Could we not procure this unique specimen to add to the JCR collection?

           Yours etc,
             JH Morley

(Trinity '57)

Yours etc,
JH Morley
(Trinity '57)

Yrs,
Bruce Coulson
(Trinity '57)

Sir,

....I am full of admiration, at the moment Sir, at your great eyesight, though of course I know you wear glasses. I can't read Mr Brogden's writing at all, and I'm sure it's "balls" anyhow. I have never seen Mr Brogden in a mood other than when he is exhaling hot air. There is a great future for him in a Turkish Bath.

Yours,
David W Blewitt

Sir,

Mr. Brogden's future, I suggest. A factor which I cannot indicate here is that the steam would appear distinctly pink, at times assuming a hue that without exaggeration might be described as bloody.

Yrs etc.
JH Morley

P.S. Mr Thomas has just come in after some sordid party, and declared that the typist is a 'bloody naked woman with tattoos on her back'.

President's reply:
What, exactly, is going on?

NR Graves
(Trinity '57)

Sir,

   Niggy-boots HAS returned – bringing with him the Asian flu' germs.

Yours etc,
JH Morley

Sir,

   Mr Graves says I'm wrong about the flu' germs. He's full of what he calls antibodies.
Yours etc,
JH Morley

President's reply:
   He should share them.

AAI Wedderburn
(Michaelmas '57)

131

Sir,

Mr. Shallcross & Mr. Harty at last take the limelight. If my drawing doesn't look like them its because they have this day become new men.

Yours etc J.H.Morley.

(Michaelmas '57)

John Morley

Honoured Sir, That blessed halycon time in England, when Good Queen Boriana, not wishing to wade openly thru the shit, stepped on VERD a fine & delicate fabric laid at her feet by a slavish admirer.

Your humble servant, J H Morley

(Hilary '58)

133

Sir,

Everybody, just everybody, ought to see Anna Magnani at the Super. I recommend this film to all & sundry, even including Brooks.

Yours JH Morley.

(Hilary '58)

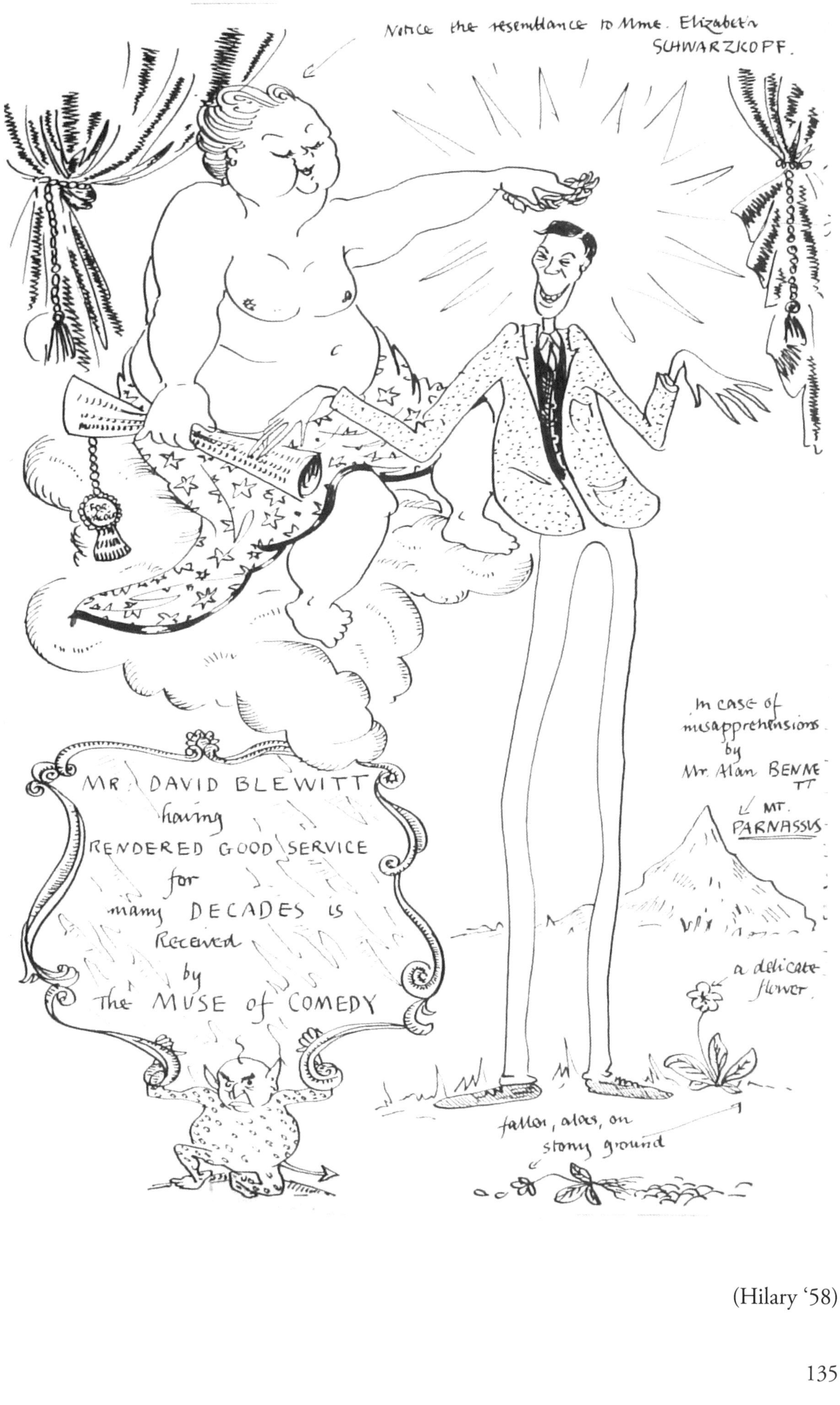
Notice the resemblance to Mme. Elizabeth SCHWARZKOPF.
MR DAVID BLEWITT having RENDERED GOOD SERVICE for many DECADES is Received by the MUSE of COMEDY
In case of misapprehensions by Mr. Alan BENNE TT
MT. PARNASSUS
a delicate flower.
fallen, alas, on stony ground

(Hilary '58)

Dear Sir,

What the book needs is a new style of

handwriting. This style seems to be the

logical one after this italic stuff, but it's

easy to see, when one is writing it, ~~why~~

Caxton was in such a hurry to introduce

the printing press.

Geoff. Chaucer (mate.)

Yrs,
John Morley
(Hilary '58)

Barnett can't think what to call this, so
I'm sure I can't.

Yrs. etc JH Morley.

(Trinity '58)

Sir,
With grateful thanks
to Mr Richard
Johnson, who told
me that the Muse
visited him last night
in the
early
hours

WANTED INSPIRATION

← [hem of the garment].

NEWDIGATE PRIZE for ENGLISH VERSE

1st class

Yrs. etc.
J H Morlay

Sir,

Perhaps Mr Johnson will tell us how to procure a visit from the Muse, before it is too late; my hopes are steadily vanishing. On the other hand, I hope I am visited by a more beautiful Muse than Mr Morley's thingummy-type – an Audrey Hepburn- type Muse would do fine.

Yrs plaintively,
JG Speirs

Sir,

With reference to the last letter, from recent and not so recent observations, surely a Judy (Hepburn or something) type muse would be more in Mr. Speirs line. Or is the word "muse" the Scottish spelling for an English "mouse"?

Yrs,
R.K. Cooke
(Hilary '58)

President's comment:

I <u>miss</u> Morley, as we all do. But I do think we ought to try and retain an accurate memory of his presence with us.

Remember for instance

The snowball he threw at the window.

Not speaking to Biny*n

The corruption of R.W. Johnson.

("I had a sort of oneness with John")

The time when I kicked him under the table to draw his attention to B.W. d'E. R. Anderson who was sitting beside him, whereupon Morley said, "What are you kicking me under the table FOR"- shouted, not said.

It is these things which keep his memory green for me.

Alan Bennett

Sir,

One more piece of Morleyana we must not forget:
"No, but you don't <u>understand</u>!"

Yrs,
D.G. Vaisey

President's comment:

There is another one which I can't actually write down. It was a sort of silence when he was about to start saying something; I suppose what's known as a pregnant silence. He'd sometimes get as far as 'B-b=b…then he'd stop.

Alan Bennett
(Michaelmas '58)

Sir,

It is quite obvious from Mr Hatch's letter that he is, as he says, "not against worship" but "is against the privileged position of worshipers (sic), in particular worshipers (sic) of the Anglican sect." He adds "fair competition in the hunt for souls." Evidently he has met with sectarian resistance.

[alias JH Morley]
(Hilary '58)

Yrsek JHMorley.

(Trinity '58)

Sir,

I would like to tell people doing schools [final exams] that when, on the second day, they think they're going to die, they won't.

Yours etc,
JH Morley

P.S. One more paper to go. Does anybody know an examiner like this – (he's always at my shoulder).

(Trinity '58)

Chapter 9
College Societies, Clubs, and Balls

One of the challenges of University life is to find an acceptable balance between working hard enough for the desired degree, and making the most of the many other opportunities available to extend existing interests, develop new ones, or merely have an enjoyable social life. Some undergraduates gave priority to College life and others to University life. This chapter focuses on College life, because that is what is reflected in the letters of the JCR Books.

The main society was the Stapeldon Society, because all undergraduates were members and contributed financially to it. But a large part of the contribution was passed down to the College's other Clubs or Societies, either as a matter of custom or practice, or because a case was made for funding a particular event. All of the sporting clubs received funding; the most expensive being The College Boat Club. Non-rowing undergraduates might be happy when the 1st Eight did well, but tended to resent the expense when it did poorly.

The John Ford Society (drama) and the College Operatic Society ("Lord Bateman" and "The Pirates of Penzance") are both mentioned in letters. Again, they tended to be mentioned when performances had been very successful or very unsuccessful. Societies like "The Paralytics" (cricket cum drinking matches) occasionally gave rise to a letter.

As regards the College balls and dances, significant sums of money were potentially at risk. The practice was to have a splendid Commemoration Ball (a Commem ball) at the end of the Trinity Term every third year, and to have a less grand Dance at the end of the Hilary Term in either or both of the intervening years. The relevant letters are in four groups, covering the Commem Ball in 1955, the Hilary Dance in 1957, the Commem Ball in 1958 and the Hilary Dance in 1959. The 1958 Commem Ball was noteworthy for the contributions of Alan Bennett and Dudley Moore, a foretaste of their later collaboration in "Beyond the Fringe".

Sir,

Do people know they can buy their TICKETS for the COMMEM BALL with POST DATED CHEQUES? 5 DAYS TO GO.

Yrs,

FWP Bentley

Sir,

The Ball.

I'm sure most of those of us who rather fancy the idea of having a Ball, would rather have one (and pay a quid as sponsors) than not have one, and pay two quid. So despite our being so far off target, let's have the Ball – we know we'll sell more later.

Now as to how to sell more tickets. I suggest: At least £10 be spent on just a couple of really decent bits of publicity. I would suggest an advertisement (small) in the Times and another (very large) in Cherwell (or if a cheaper rate is offered, in Isis). And if possible, get the news of the thing to... any and everybody who writes or says anything which anyone reads. If necessary fake a stunt – but do get the Ball talked about, if possible nationally. While we are unlikely to sell a hundred tickets to (say) Constance Spry's usual audience, there is a very real chance that elderly or other graduates will read of a commem with nostalgia and, casting prejudice to the winds, will send off for a dozen tickets for ours.

Yours earnestly,

V. Denis Vandervelde

Sir,

Mr Vandervelde is very helpful – but we are not primarily worried about the absence of outsiders. It is ridiculous that a college of 270 undergraduates should muster only 66 for the Ball – just under one quarter.

We have, incidentally, advertised more in The Times and Cherwell than any other Ball.

Yrs etc,

Brian Brindley

Sir,

The whole fabric of the College is crumbling!

I have seen no less than EIGHT different young ladies in the Front Quad in the last ten minutes.

Can the place be looking up?

Yrs,

FWP Bentley

Sir,

May I through the medium of your columns correct Mr Bentley, or rather suggest that more relevantly, in the words of the Sunday Times special correspondent (damn him for his Wadham leanings) "Gardens yield themselves languorously behind stone walls and colleges crumble like Wensleydale cheese."

Yours etc,

PM Lewis

(Trinity '55)

Sir,

Could we have some statement about the bands who are going to play at this Hilary Dance? I have been horrified to hear that the only music is to come from two undergraduate bands. This is just not good enough for two guineas. I believe I am right in saying that the last Hilary Ball and the Commem both made profits. We have had enough of this "Empire-building" and "Saving for future generations" stuff. If we are to be asked for two guineas we want two guineas worth of value. The most important thing by far is a bloody good band. Any idea of free drink, or extra food should be scrapped.

It is hopeless hiring an unknown band, setting a low budget and then declaring that any tickets after the break-even point will be re-invested. If you build on a small-scale, you can only add to the building in a limited way. Could we please have some imaginative and bold planning, and for goodness' sake – a decent, well-known band.

Yours,
Peter Jackson

President's reply:

I think you are labouring under a large misapprehension. Any band we could have hired for the dance would have been an amateur band. This has always been the case in the past. There is no cheeseparing involved here; you might have made enquiries before you started making silly accusations. At the last Hilary Dance the undergraduate band was infinitely better than the so called professional one – and I am quite confident that the 2 bands we have – the O.U. Jazz Band playing traditional Jazz and the Ambassadors playing sambas, quicksteps etc – will be excellent.

Nor is there any question of making a profit – that is the point of the notice – that we should be able to plough back the profits – and incidentally the idea of making a profit on the Hilary Ball has simply been to offset the losses on the Commems. It just happens that this last year we made a profit.

When I put up a notice asking for volunteers for the dance I shall expect your name to stand high on the list – we will need some imaginative people to help take up the floor at 4 am.

Alan Bennett

Sir,

I am surprised to find that as yet there has been no comment here on the Hilary Ball. Since there is no "I told you so," I assume that others feel as I do, that it was a first-class evening and that all those who aided the organisation should be warmly thanked and congratulated.

SR Merrett
(Hilary '59)

Sir,

May we hire the Malc Brown High Steppers for bashful men at the Hilary Dance?

Yrs,

DA Whitelock

17 Upper Windmill St, W1

Dear Mr. Whitelock,

Thank you for your enquiry of the 14th inst. I am most gratified to hear of the recommendation of us by His Grace, whom we have had the honour to oblige on numerous occasions.

Would you require my No. 1 troupe, 'The Brown Hatters' ('Leggy, luscious, lascivious' .....The Tablet;) or my hand-picked corps of hostess/entertainers, the 'Brownie Patrol' who are so popular a feature at the Thursday club?

Yrs. sincerely,

Malcolm Brown

(p.p. Messina Typing Agency Ltd.)

[Hurry, hurry, hurry guys!! You Oxford eggheads ain't never gonna see anything like these superdooper heybobarebop girlies when they hit yore neck of the woods! Yes siree, when me 'n' the cuties cut a rug we reely hack it!! With the Eddie Bedson Hot Ten Platelayers, and Eric Kemp and his close harmony Bible Bashers. Hurry! Hurry! Hurry! Tickets from Ace in the Hole Spathis. I'll be a seein' yew kids!]

[Signed Malc (bring yore problems to me, dish) Brown
(Actually DA Whitelock)]

Mifter Mᶜˡᵐ Brovvn, GENT.

Has the honor to announce to all Gentlefolk who feek

Entertainers

for

Mafkes,   Routes,
Madrigals,   Feaftes,
        Revels,

That his Trained and Truftworthy Troop of

Wenches of Eafe

May be had by addrefs to his agent

Mifter Thos. Befwick Siſſons,

*at the Signe of the Goat~with~
Horne,
in Saint Giles Walke.*

(Hilary '57)

147

Sir,

What I want to know is – what happens to Lord Bateman and Sophia in the interval between the end of the second Act and the beginning of the Third?

Yrs,

R.W. Johnson

President's reply:

I thought you knew all about that sort of thing.

Alan Bennett

Sir,

What I do know is what Lord Bateman does to Sophia between Act II, Scene 2 and Scene 3; it's horrible, Sir.

Yours,

M. Woodgett

President's reply:

Come, come. This is a Victorian outlook. We must, as I have often said from the pulpit, get used to the fact that sex is a part – and a very real and important part – (but still only a part) – of life.

Alan Bennett

Sir,

Watch the orchestra playing the music in between these two scenes … it's quite sensual!

Yrs,

Tracey [Andrew Tracey]

President's reply:

I noticed the bassoonist doing something with his instrument though my view was obscured by the Lady Mayoress of Oxford's hat.

Alan Bennett

Sir,

It's a matter, really, of what Sophia does to Lord Bateman, not the other way round.

Yours,

Lord Bateman (Bart)

[MA Sharpe]

P.S. My affairs are conditioned by heirs, and I must perforce populate my feudal state. What should I do?

President's reply:

I think if you proceed empirically along the lines of what I saw on the stage you will eventually reach a conclusion.

Alan Bennett
(Michaelmas '58)

Sir,

I see there is a ban on commercials: but this is merely an advertisement. Take a trip along to Walton St, Moaters, and see 'The Pirates' – it's quite good news: the girls are quite presentable, and the chaps in the Policemen's Chorus are very funny indeed. All they need is a large audience to laugh at 'em: so on you go, all you Ruggermen, rowing-men, dartsmen (for Johnson R.W.'s sake), chaps et al.

The opera is only on till FRIDAY, this week.

Yrs,

The Duke of Plazatoro
(J.G. Speirs)

Sir,

The Pirates is really rather good news – recommended for all the family, chaps etc. As a matter of fact one of the secondary leads is very smooth (female one, I mean). You are strongly advised to get tickets NOW.

'Absolutely splendid.'	The Senior Tutor
'As Good as Doily Cart!'	A large puddingish woman in green.
'Bloody.'	M Woodgett

M Woodgett
(Michaelmas '59)

Dear Sir,

Do you know Miss Theodora Parfit (19) of Somerville College? She says, in the "Woman's Mirror" Oct 23, page 13 – "I recommend trial marriages only for the more intelligent people. I don't think they would be a good thing for the working classes. After all, working-class teenagers live at home and don't have much money, so my ideas would be difficult for them to try... Besides... they could not possibly appreciate the subtleties of the relationship I suggested. All my friends at the University agree with me, but then, I have always associated with intelligent people." She goes on to say that, "there's no point in preaching if you don't have the courage to put your convictions into practice."

How about the Adelphi Club – or any suitable collection of the chaps (i.e. male, part of the non-working classes) – inviting Miss Parfit to dine and to find a suitable partner?

Just the thing for a smoothie who's pushed, what?

Yours,

JM Ashworth
(Michaelmas '59)

Sir,

I felt too bloody, when I surfaced finally at 1pm today, to say what a 'splendid' show Exeter put up yestreen; but now dear old Culver tells me to give his thanks to the Committee for their grand effort. I think we should thank him for grinding the organ so well himself. I am feeling very sad: I have just parted for 3 and a half months with a fond farewell – in fact I am almost weeping with despondency, so feel for me, Sir.

Goodbye, have a good vac, Zander my boy.

Yrs (lovelornly),
JGS [Speirs]

P.S. I am too shy to sign my name properly.

Sir,

More Moore for the boys, eh? Add an odd spot of Dankworth et femme for fill in and I reckon you could have quite a little get together.

After the ball is over, after the drizzling dawn
None of the boys are sober, all of the booze is gone.
Marge has gone back to the stillroom, Speirs has lovelornly gone down,
Zander is wielding a stiff broom, the lawn's gone brown.

With apologies for scribble,
Yrs,
Lyrical Len
(Trinity '58)

Sir,

Speaking of brothels (Hoppy was) and as the BALL suggestions book appears to have become lost, I would like to bring this idea to your attention,. Why not send a small bus to London on the evening before our little affair, and bring a stack of real, live, very high class whores up to Oxford, to grace the occasion. This, I feel sure, would make Exeter's Commem the highlight of the social season.

Yrs etc,
T.E. Smith
(Hilary '58)

Sir, 'Mr. Smith makes me feel profoundly uneasy. He wants to make a nightclub in a vault [with a sandy soil floor]. He is emphatic that this should be completed in time for the Commem. And his latest suggestion is that strange whores should be brought into the district for the occasion.

Are his motives entirely above suspicion? We all know Mr. Smith.

Yrs. etc. J H Morley.

P.S. There must be no stains in this College that cannot be removed with an ordinary detergent.

(Hilary '58)

Sir,

Depression fell on the tense knot of Little Sprojham supporters. The Major buried his face in twitching hands. 6 left to get to win, "Demon" Coulson bumping them like fury, and only a complete stranger to go in as eleventh! Graves was still there, true, and batting like a good 'un, but that last ripsnorter from "Demon" had obviously knocked out several teeth. He was brave, brave, but weakening visibly. "Aht beant a arpoth o use sitha appen," muttered Old Ben, pulling tensely on his reeking corncob. "Just when we had Upper Belchin on the run, too, for the first time in years!" rapped Captain Thomas, gripping his portable steering wheel till the knuckles showed white. Only Wells-Furby said nothing, his eyes puckering shrewdly beneath thoughtful brows as he watched young Spathis walk out to the pitch. "By George, that chap looks clean cut," he said. "A sound second I bet, and well plucked…"

Froth flies from Demon Coulson's teeth as he sprints viciously at the wicket: his bronzed arm flails, the ball screams at Young Spathis's well-groomed figure. But ho there; those wide shoulders open: a flash, the sweet, English crack of willow and leather! High wide and handsome the 'Spathine Six' (as it goes down in Oxfordshire legend) wings effortlessly across the empyrean, knocks the weathervane askew on the ancient Little Spronjham church, strips three yards of lead from the vicarage roof, bounces in Squire Close's orchid hothouses, and brains the vicar as he sports among the raspberry canes with the barmaid from the Baron of Beef. An amazed din rises from the pavilion. Old Ben has apoplexy and drops dead on the spot. Graves does a tango and cheers himself hoarse. The Major goes off his head. Young Spathis peels off his batting gloves and grins modestly. And Wells-Furby? "Stout show!" says he.

Yrs,
DA Whitelock
(Trinity '57)

Chapter 10
Politically Incorrect

Malcolm Brown and Bruce Coulson both went up to Exeter in 1954 and both made their mark in College. Malcolm was an entertaining member of the JCR and as a result was elected Millerian Professor, a post for which he was ideally qualified. The attached letters give an idea of the versatility he brought to his writing, which is apparent in the numerous other letters scattered throughout this book. He could also turn his hand to amusing drawings, for example his before and after state of the ladies' loo in Chapter 7 as a result of his campaign to have it improved.

Bruce Coulson was much more of a Jekyll and Hyde character, as implied in Malcolm's amusing letter to "Dear Bruce Blue-eyes" in the first part of this chapter. This was in response to four pages of illegible fury on Bruce's part. The problem was that in the late evening after having drink-taken, he had to be thwarted from doing the JCR Book an injury (being thrown round the room or having pages torn out). However he was also courteous, amusing, well-informed and well-read. Both sides of his character are represented in the JCR Books.

It should not be forgotten that Exeter College in the 1950s was still an all-male college. As National Service only ended in 1960, most of the undergraduates had spent two years since leaving school in one of the Services. The JCR Books reflect the strong male environment and the more politically incorrect nature of that period. This chapter includes some rude and vulgar letters and limericks.

Sir,

Mr. Roper has gone to London on a dirty weekend. This is his third dirty weekend in ten days!!! Surely, sir, we ought to protect him from himself? Not only is he letting slip his chance of a brilliant 4th in Schools, but he is losing track of time – one of the well-known symptoms of the third and Virulent Stage of that disease so carefully explained to us by the Army Kinema Corporation. Who knows what permanent harm he is doing himself on these lust-crazed excursions to the Metropolis? Sir, Save Roper!

Yours with genuine concern,
Malcolm Brown
(Trinity '56)

⚊ ⚊

Sir,

Here's a poem to fill out the book:

> The chief defect of Nigel Graves
> Was taking damsels into caves
>
> And here beside the shimmering sea
> He'd gently take them on his knee,
>
> And stroke their lovely pubic hair
> And wonder, at the same time, where
>
> And why or who, and sometimes what,
> And whether it was right or not,--
>
> But, really, questions such as these
> Weren't calculated Nige to please.
>
> So as the sun sank in the West
> He'd strip down to his Aertex vest,
>
> Leaving, of course, his pants, Y-Front.

PH Lewis and Michael H. Imison

President's reply:

> The chief defect of Lewis, P.
> Was asking people out to tea,
> Then, finding that he had no food,
> And not desiring to be rude,
> To LMH he'd ask them round,
> Where, to his embarrassment, he found…

To be continued
Nigel Graves

Sir,

You say you wish us all to see
The chief defect of Lewis P.
But pray you must be kind and tell
How when where and to whom he fell.

Yours etc.
JP Partridge

Sir,

Whenever gentlemen peruse
The never ending, puerile muse
That seems to over fill this book,
They soon sit down and start to look
Around for words that almost rhyme
And oft find some, but, then, in time,
They end up with a line going something like this one.

Yrs,
RC Hennessy

Sir,

Young Hennesie a plant peruser
Turns into a critic
Of poet, muser, shady boozer,
Rhymster paralytic.
Though up to now he never knew it
He must pay the price
Though he may rue it Mr. Blewitt
Thinks he's rather nice.

Yrs etc.
Brucie (B.W. Coulson)
(Trinity '57)

Sir,

A reflection on College Food, which occurred to me in a dream:
A young nymphomaniac Cretan
Felt her sexiest after she'd eaten.
Each night after supper,
She had all of them up'er.
A dessert unprescribed by la Beeton.

Yours with balls,
Michael J. Crowe

President's reply:

Now that's what I would call a dream.

John Moat
(Hilary '60)

⌒

Sir,

In Palmer's Green
La belle poitrine
Lies all too often fallow:
Unlike the curves
That one observes
In Rome – or in Rapallo.

Oh, you can trust
The foreign bust
To thrust itself well forward:
A charming trait
Which, sad to say,
Is lacking in West Norwood.

In Budapest
The female breast
Is looked on as an asset:
A point of view
Which is taboo
In Bath, or Wootton Bassett.

Yrs plagiaristically
David Garrood
(Trinity '56)

⌒

Sir,

...   Patience Strong writes:

Here, for all my readers is another beautiful thought for their anthologies.

Marcel Proust had a very poor figure
He hadn't the chest for sexual rigour.
He lay with Albertine tout nu;
'Ce n'est seulement le temps qu'il a perdu'

Alan Bennett
(Hilary '57)

⌒

Sir,

Time was when heroes walked the hallowed ground of this college. As Mr Hall (K) says, 'This is like a bloody dingy club, with a load of old men lying about reading papers.' And I agree with this to some extent. It is just one more symptom. The whole blasted place is dead (from the toenails up), wholly dead.

My god! What a goddam dive! A few seedy trogs. Slightly more drunken, run of the mill rotten syph-ridden drunken clots, and what else, I ask you [?] Malc with an indifferent, and I with no, audience. Fuck it! Colourless, a colourless toneless buzz in the bastard background.

Oh, god! Time was when heroes, heroic chaps with style and a certain obscene dignity livened our marvelling senses with the dazzle and the chivalry, of such activity of mind and heart and stomach, as will, if what I fear, believe me with due cause, is true will never more be seen, or heard of.

Oh Hell! Which side off-sett is the goddam and fucking blasted fore-sight of –shit-a –bren{n} Gun.

What depths of cretinosity are we fell to? And now they've all gone. Nothing, blast it, but a turdish silence punctuated by the heavy breathing of Geronimo Spathis, who occasionally whispers- yes- queer thing in by lug. Oh Fuck, yes I mean it, Sir, but will not repeat it lest the unsavourory, harsh, syllable, offend, your soft and chaste and ill-acquainted ear.

I am so overcome I cannot speak.

Yours etc,
Bruce William Coulson (future BA perhaps)

Dear "Bruce Blue-Eyes",

Your letter interested me very much, and I showed it to our own graphologist, Professor Zara. He tells me that your handwriting shows great character and imagination, but that you are a very sensitive and easily downcast personality, not at home in the harsh everyday world. And, my dear, are you just the teeniest bit given to excess in seeking release from your worries? The way you form your 'f's and your 'c's shows a strongly developed artistic trait, which you should cultivate. Why not join an evening class for pottery or lace-making, anything which will provide you with a harmless outlet for your energies?

As to your other query, (only one 'e', dear,) what you fear is hardly likely, though you could ask your doctor.

Yours very sincerely,
Mary Brown (Malcolm Brown)
(Hilary '57)

Sir,

With reference to the correspondence regarding the differences between black and white ones last term, could Malc [Malcolm Brown] explain the subtle difference implied below

---

Hello Boys!

Come to
Irene's Beer Gardens
51 Highholborn Street, Kingston
Wine, Dinc, Dance, Romance and thrill
With White, French and Chinese Girls
To the fun provided at your request
BEST ACCOMODATION

Yours sincerely,
M. Seakins

Sir,

The difference between white girls is enormous, especially in Huddersfield.
French girls are not all white. (Vide. O.F. 'chansonette')
"O dis-moi, Marianne
Je voudrais bien savoir
Pourquoi les femmes blondes
Ont les xxxxx noirs."
The difference between Chinese girls is that they are all the same.
Yrs,
Malc.(Malcolm Brown)
(Hilary '58)

158

Sir,

Did you know we have a counterpart in Oxford to the "Rose-Pink Ballet"? I bet Mr. Rose has never told you about his "Cherwell Changelings" (presented by arrangement with the late Mr. Vandervelt for the delectation of elderly dons) so-called after a number in which the young girls dress and undress behind a copy of "Cherwell" (although once Eric Kemp [College Chaplain] made them use the "Church Times" instead, in spite of Mr. Rose's protests that it destroyed the literary allusion). At the critical moment one of the gentlemen approaches and sets fire to the paper (of course he has to pay heavily for the privilege). When these performances had become well known in certain circles somebody (Mr. Millet?) took some of the acts over to Paris, and when he was searching for a suitable name, not unnaturally the first thing that occurred to him was "Les Ballets Roses". I think this monster ought to be exposed, sir.

Yrs, etc,
Defensor Juventutis [Mr Shobbrook]

P.S. Did he have official permission? I don't know, but when I was secretly observing the proceedings I saw the Proctors and Bulldogs standing watching, clad only in gowns, mortarboards, and bowlers, as appropriate.

President's reply:

On the contrary he has told me <u>All</u> about them. Frequently. And I may say you have got only half the story. If that. However, Mr. Rose must be treated charitably. He is a sick man. Tout comprendre c'est tout pardonner. He may look like you – or – well – or me, I suppose – but he isn't really. Deep down he's different. He's not the same. Banish all thoughts of 'official permission', 'preventive action'. Live with him, talk to him, get to know him. Help him. It's the only way. And please Mr. Shobbrook, sign your letters. <u>You</u> have nothing to be ashamed of.

Alan Bennett
(Michaelmas '58)

Sir,

I must say – and may this once and for all clear up all doubts about St. Hilda's – that that college does of course provide for each girl a sturdy wooden chair, for chaps to hang their trousers on, and furthermore for use in some of the more technically involved positions which are still practised in this ancient seat of learning. We all know of course the anatomical details which Mr. Sweet has seen fit to supply us with (these in fact of el positiono Spanisho – the ole position). So of course does the Principal of St. Hilda's; and the whole question of performing it <u>in bed</u> not only causes bad bed-linen form, but constitutes a gross contravention of Positional Shaping Form for which surely no one could be excused.

Wilbur

Sir,

I offer a prize of ales (two) for the man who produces the best conclusion to the following limerick opening:

There was a young bird from St Hilda's,
Who, while shaping, was seen by some builders
Etc

Entries to 'Piece by end of 7th Wk: entries to be judged by 'Piece and Badecoke.

Yrs Aye,
'Piece

Sir,

Variation on a theme:

There was a young bird of St. Hilda
Who shaped once in bed with a builder;
He said that he would,
And he could, and he should,
And he did, and he bloody near killed her.

Yrs,
Millerian Prof.

Sir,

There was a young bird from St. Hilda's
Who, while shaping, was seen by some builders.
When they cried, "What a t*rd!"
She said, "Don't be absurd –
I'm an elegant bird from St. Hilda's!"

Yrs,
JD Winter

Sir,

> There was a young girl from St. Hilda's
> Who – while shaping – was seen by some builders.
> She said, "This man's meat
> Is like a tadpole on heat:
> What I want is a good flash of Wilbur's."

Sir,

> There was a young girl from St. Hilda's
> Who, while shaping, was seen by some builders.
> She preferred it in bed,
> With EEK's, so she said,
> Being longer and stronger than Wilbur's.

David Seconde

Sir,

There's a wind of challenge in the air these days. Accordingly:

> There was a young bird of St. Hilda's
> Who, while shaping, was seen by some builders.
> Now, once penetrated,
> She was not to be sated,
> But in twenty man-hours they had filled her.

> There was a young bird from St.Hilda's,
> Who while shaping was seen by some builders.
> She wasn't much gladder
> When had on a ladder,
> 'Twas the plumb and the trowels that thrilled her.

RP Bolkeley

Sir,

> There was a young bird from St. Hilda's,
> Who, while shaping, was seen by some builders.
> She was able to stick
> The hard-core and brick,
> But 10 yards of piping just killed her.

MW Bastin
(Michaelmas '60)

Yrs etc,
Brucie (Bruce Coulson)
(Hilary '57)

Chapter 11
College Animals

The early letters refer to the College cats, in the plural, and Mr Whitelock's (Derek Whitelock, 1954) goldfish, Hengist. Thereafter the focus is on one cat only, the College chef's notorious Carruthers, against whom Alan Bennett waged a long campaign, with the support of many other undergraduates. There was also a long-lived tortoise in the College garden, which is joined by a mythical alligator in a splendid series of four letters and three replies from the President Nigel Graves, accompanied by Bruce Coulson's fine drawing of the alligator, with the Spectator under its arm.

Unfortunately many splendid stories did not appear in the JCR Books. Sam Eadie (1954-1958), who was regularly elected Millerian Professor, has recalled two tales about his contemporary, Memo Spathis. Memo had told some friends that his (female) hamster needed a mate, so they bought a male in the Market and were promised a refund of their 2/6 (2 shillings and 6 pence) if they brought it back. However, Memo's hamster fought off the male and escaped, only to surface at High Table much later under the eyes of a College Fellow, who was alleged to have attributed the apparition to an excess of port, which he then renounced for the next fortnight.

On another occasion, Memo had lent his large room overlooking the Front Quad to the Opera Society, who left it after a party in such a mess that the scout (cleaner) called the Sub-Rector to see the mess for himself. They were confronted by Memo's cat, who was finishing up all the dregs and had clearly become quite intoxicated. The Sub-Rector told Memo that the cat would not be sent down immediately but would be advised not to return the following term.

Sir,

When, with a weeping soul, I tipped Hengist into the pond, I trusted that he would be safe and happy. But, Sir, today I cannot see him anywhere. What has happened to the little Fellow? What Finny Fiend lurks in that pond? What devilry is Afoot. Along with other right-thinking fish-lovers of this college I demand an investigation. A thought occurs to me. Let us put Mr. Short in the pond for the night to solve the mystery.

Yrs,

DA Whitelock

President's comment:

This is very sad indeed. The Sub-rector and the police will be informed. The Sub-rector will probably lurk in the tree overhanging the pond and pounce on the monster the next time he strikes. But a little bait, as you say, would be useful.

SK Guram

Sir,

IN MEMORIAM
of Hengist
Prince of Goldfish who
Departed this Life circa early March 1955 under Dreadful Conditions
Will always be remembered by Derek, Ben, Adrian, Parters and
Uncle Brian
"GONE BUT NOT FORGOTTEN"
Yrs etc,
Brian Brindley
(Hilary '55)

Sir,

How delicate, how rare, how passing fair it is to hear the drowsy cooing of the doves on the chapel roof, conjuring up as it does in the hearkener's mind vistas of scented pines and blossoming boskage, walled gardens in high summer with gauzy-winged bees buzzing 'mid the nasturtia, and divers delectations! Let us make the college into a compleat pleasaunce with a fish pond fill'd with wondrous carp, in which piscatorial alumni, couched on nectarous kingcup beds beneath the willows, may cast their leisur'd flies. Fallow deer will tread delicately over the sward, jewel-ey'd shrews disport themselves in the herbage, while from the steeple comes the burbling call of the quagfinch (quesorialis cerax cerax)

> Yrs.
> DA Whitelock
> (Hilary '56)

Sir,

Since all attempts to grow grass on the lawn are bound to be foiled by Carruthers, the only course open is to dig up the lawn, and replace it with cobbles. Carruthers could cross the road and shit on Jesus lawn; we would all save any amount of time and energy by being able to walk straight across the quad.

> Yrs etc,
> NR Graves
> (Hilary '56)

Sir,

Mr Bennett says that Carruthers is still making marks on the grass. Let's give him/her a cat-tin, sir, ... full of sand, so that visitors will think it's a fire-bucket, and only we and Carruthers will know what's really in it, until we have a fire,

> Yours etc,
> A Bedson

Sir,

The bald patches on the lawn in the Front Quad look horrible. For goodness sake have Carruthers put to sleep; at least do something.

> Yrs,
> M. Woodgett

Sir,

Oh God! Not a fertile Carruthers!

> Malc (Brown)

Sir,

This cat problem ought to be taken seriously. Everyone seems to agree on two points viz (a) the cat ought to be eliminated; (b) the chef is too good to lose.

At the moment these two factors appear to be incompatible or to put it another way, you can't have your cat and eat it. This situation seems to crop up in a slightly different form in numerous 'thrillers' where the standard way out seems to contrive the desired elimination by an apparent accident. Seen in this light the problem is simple and there are numerous possibilities:

1) a road accident, cunningly involving a Jesus car
2) a large, starved rat and a tethered Carruthers

3) a sadistic female with a cat complex (see S Romer for details)

4) a visit by a food inspector

5) ditto an official of the RSPCA

6) a gang of Liverpool cat slingers etc etc etc

Yours,

JM Ashworth

Sir,

Can we really take this Carruthers business seriously? The only way to get rid of it is to take it to some distant point by car and chloroform it and put it in a dustbin. There are two possible times when this could be done without the chef knowing:

1) 1pm when he is doling out the soup

2) 7pm when he is doling out the soup (probably the same soup, but hey ho!).

Someone's got to do the deed – some members of the SCR incidentally think the business is a farce, and wouldn't I'm sure say no. Another way would be to call in the Sanitary Inspectors, tell them what Marge says about its activities in the kitchen, and that might do the trick.

I understand there is a vociferous and small body of opinion headed by an unlikely duo, Messrs Lewis and Shobbrook, who want to retain it as an institution. This plea must be ignored. No false sentimentality must interfere with the doing of the deed. And now (this ought to be in the other book) when food is at its nadir should the deed be done – not as an act of vengeance but of expiation.

Yrs etc,

A Bennett

P.S. If anyone has an uneasy conscience on this matter we could send a subscription to the RSPCA.

Sir,

I am sorry to see other matters have distracted attention from the annihilation of Carruthers. The matter is no less urgent than it was last week: tonight Stambach found 3 hairs in his omelette – two of them were undoubtedly feline, and one of them, equally undoubtedly, pubic. Speirs thereupon found a further hair in his gooseberry (sic) pie. It is, in the immortal capitals of BDFTB, TOO BAD. Something must be done. Mrs Wheare (the Rector's wife) was asking me today what the patches were. I hardly had the heart to tell her. She thought it was because gentlemen stood on the lawn. They have a cat now. Would you please make representations to her:

1) That they have it neutered-doctored – anyway put out of action from a sexual point of view (otherwise we're going to be overrun and shat on from all quarters.)

2) That it only craps, if crap it must, on their lawn not on ours.

Yrs etc,

Alan Bennett

(Hilary '58)

A Ballet in One Act.

Characters.: The Young Man.
                    The Cat.

Sir,

I LOVE little Pussy

OVEN

Her coat is SO warm,

P.T.O.

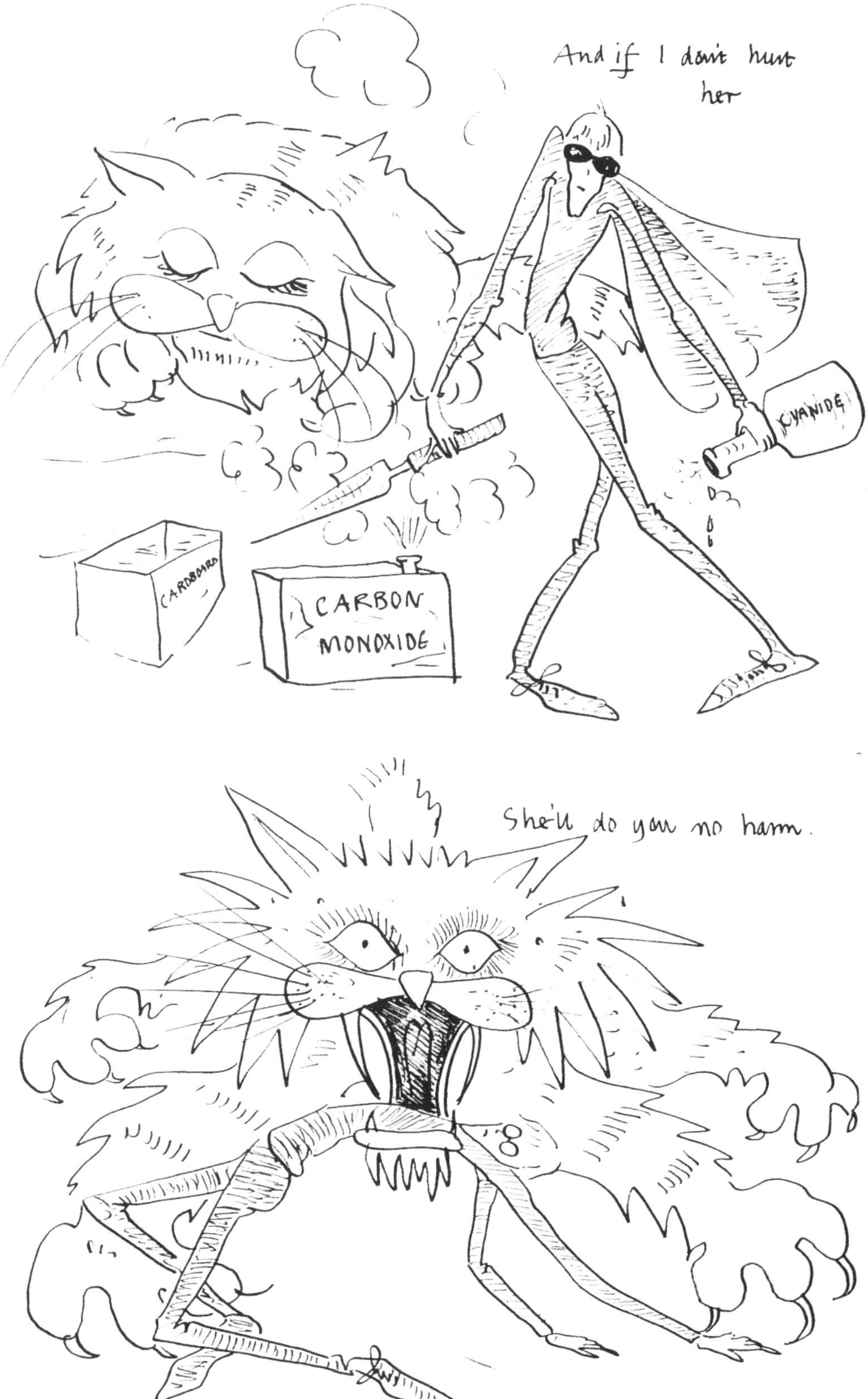
And if I don't hurt her
CARDBOARD
CARBON MONOXIDE
CYANIDE
She'll do you no harm.

Yrs,

John Morley

(Spring '58)

Sir,

The varied views of the college, are, to copy an eminent colleague of mine, readily described as "amorphous". To the best of my knowledge – and this includes my more inebriated moments – I have never seen either a tortoise or an alligator/crocodile in the College garden.

Yours,

DW Blewitt

President's reply

The tortoise is a good friend of mine, but I have never met the alligator.

NR Graves

Sir,

he hasn't, but I have:–

Yours etc,

BW Coulson

President's reply

I stand corrected – I have met him.

NR Graves

Sir,

There is a tortoise in the college garden. I saw it telling Mr Bennett that joke about the lively post-Restoration Rector John Yorricks Prideaux, who was Rector for a few days in the summer of 1661. At least Mr Bennett appeared very interested in this senior member of the college (the tortoise). But what is its name? her name? his name?

Yrs,

H Inselberg

Sir,

Mr. Coulson's mind seems recently to run almost exclusively on reptiles. What do you think is the significance of this horrid preoccupation?

Yrs etc.,

JH Morley

President's reply:

He merely follows in your footsteps.

NR Graves

(Trinity '57)

SIR,

PERHAPS SOME KIND GENTLEMEN WOULD CARE TO CONTRIBUTE TOWARDS A FUND FOR FORMING AN EXETER COLLEGE MENAGERIE?

YOURS ETC.,

R. W. JOHNSON.
(Morley Type)

(Hilary '58)

Index by Name

*The letter 'm' after a page reference indicates that the person is merely mentioned or drawn by someone else, and is not the author of the extract.